LITTLE OLD MAN
CUT SHORT

Cover picture by Gerry O Donovan shows Fleet Street in 1960. The Author in his Berkley sports car, deciding whether to go to work or have a drink.

LITTLE OLD MAN
CUT SHORT

Donal O'Donovan

Donal O'Donovan (signature)

KB
Kestrel Books

© for text - Donal O'Donovan
© for typesetting, cover design, layout - Kestrel Books Ltd.

ISBN: 1 900505 90 8

Published 1998 by Kestrel Books Ltd.
48A Main St., Bray, Co. Wicklow, Ireland.
Tel: +353 1 286 3402; Fax: +353 1 286 0984

Printed in Ireland by Falcon Print & Finish Ltd.

CONTENTS

CHAPTER 1

LAUREL LODGE

At first I was not the eldest: I was the only. My parents were in the 1920s not alone in being middle class and poor. Those who chose the wrong side in the Civil War paid the price, and my father's M.Sc. was of little use in a State that gave the victors the spoils.

My parents, one a retired Director of Chemicals on the General Staff of the Irish Republican Army, the other a flapper not long out of school at Loreto on the Green, were not I think especially well matched. Their common bond was the Republican movement (my mother was a sister of Kevin Barry) but there was nine years' difference in their ages and my mother used to tell me that she had been foolish to marry at 20. That was in 1926. They made a handsome couple but there are no wedding photographs. For some unfathomable reason they ducked their own wedding reception in the Grosvenor Hotel across the road from St. Andrew's, Westland Row, and took an early boat train for Brussels. It was one of many incidents that the family did not bring up in conversation.

In January 1928, I was in a hurry to come into the world. Or the doctor was late. At any rate I was born at home in 8 Upper Cherryfield Avenue in the Dublin suburb of Ranelagh, one of fourteen fixed abodes that my parents were to rent or buy (they only bought twice) in the south side of Dublin.

When I say they, I mean him. My mother was not usually consulted about moves until decisions had been made. I remember how upset she was when we left Florenceville, the house we bought in 1937 and sold ten years later.

I do not possess a good memory, but I recall flashes of my first years. Visiting my paternal grandparents in Drumcondra not long before they died in 1930 and 1931; being driven around Dublin in my Corkonian Aunt Bridie's Model A Ford to see the preparations - window-boxes and papal flags - for the Eucharistic Congress of 1932, when a million people gathered in the Phoenix Park and heard Count John McCormack sing *Panis Angelicus*. Playing with my sister Mary in a sand-filled garden shed at the back of 6 St. Edward's Terrace, Rathgar. Mary left my life soon afterward. She died in 1933, aged four. My father told me years afterwards that after they planted her in Dean's Grange Cemetery my parents went to Sandymount Strand and held hands. It was perhaps the only private personal thing he ever told me.

One or two houses later, in Fairfield Park, Rathgar, I played or fought with my coeval Ulick O'Connor and his toy train. He lived - still does - in No. 15: we were in No.9. I recall running away from home and being found in Palmerston Park; stealing a copper from the kitchen mantelpiece and buying a packet of sweet cigarettes; being allowed to accompany Leverett and Frye's van man on his grocery rounds until I fell out and hurt myself.

By then I had a younger brother, Gerry, and a new sister Sheila, and we got our first family car, a Model Y Ford ("Baby Ford"). My father had at last got a job, in the new State company that supplied the country with electric power from the Shannon Scheme at Ardnacrusha and I think the car went with the job.

In a way he was using his M.Sc. in chemistry, devising and supervising the paints for the giant pylons that were marching up the mountains and across the plains of Ireland to form the national grid. The Electricity Supply Board was to be his mainstay until he retired in 1961, but his was a restless spirit and he spent much of his leisure time in more rewarding if troublesome pursuits.

My brother Gerry developed tuberculosis, then and up to 1950 a national scourge. After he spent some time in Cappagh Hospital, Jim and Monty (my parents: let me introduce you) decided to take a house in the country. Laughable so to describe Ballybrack now, but country it was then, a sleepy village with some big houses and large farms with fields facing the Leadmines at Ballycorus. That was where John Dowling the Republican leader, dentist, artist and art critic, painted many of his landscapes. "Haystacks Dowling", we called him.

From Laurel Lodge, Ballybrack, I first went to school in Bray. I took the bus to St. Brigid's on Duncairn Terrace, where they made me write with my right hand and prepared me for my First Holy Communion. The priest was Dr. Edward O'Brien, then curate in charge of St. Peter's, Little Bray, and close friend (though I did not know it until my student days) of my uncle Dan O'Donovan. Two years earlier, Garret FitzGerald began his schooling with the same Misses Brayden. My cousin Ruth Brennan was there with me, and apart from those two and Tommy Corcoran and Kenneth Brayden, a nephew of the teachers, I recall nobody. Nor, it must be said, do I remember any unpleasantness in that tranquil place.

At home there were stormier events. One night before our party guests were due to arrive, the wind blew so hard that it pushed in the kitchen window and we had to use the table to keep the storm at bay. Then one day, after Farmer Duffy next door had saved the hay and filled his big barn with it, his two sons and I found a haybogey upended against the hay and began to play house in the dark space. A house is not a house without a light, so I,

At Laurel Lodge, Ballybrack, in 1934. My paternal aunt Min is holding Gerry, Mother has Sheila.

the eldest, fetched a book of matches from home. The wisp of hay that stuck out burned brightly and seconds later the conflagration began. A thousand pounds' worth of hay, the bogey and the barn went up, and I hid under the stairs until my father came home. The Dún Laoghaire fire brigade spent three days fighting the flames and had some trouble getting water from the stream down the field. I got my photograph in the *Evening Herald* and in spite of whatever punishment I received, I enjoyed my moment in the sun. Whenever I smell burning leaves it brings back a warm memory.

Here in this house, my younger sister Aedine was born. Not born: in those days middle-class Dublin women had their children in one of the nursing homes around Hatch Street. But I first met her in Laurel Lodge, and in spite of the nine years between us we are still good friends.

I should explain Monty's unlikely name. She was baptised Mary (hence my dead sister). She became a more fashionable Maureen; then at school Mon B. (for Barry); Monby, Monty. Jim to add to the confusion, always called her Monny, his pet name for her.

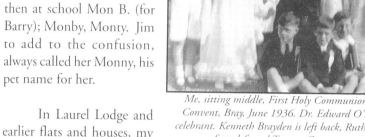

Me, sitting middle, First Holy Communion, Ravenswell Convent, Bray, June 1936. Dr. Edward O'Brien was the celebrant. Kenneth Brayden is left back, Ruth Brennan sixth from left and Tommy Corcoran to my left.

In Laurel Lodge and earlier flats and houses, my mother and I formed a close friendship. She taught me rebel songs and "The Isle of Capri"; she made me sing the *Marseillaise* until I got the difficult melody right; she offered me the daily snipe of Guinness (half a bottle) that was prescribed for her as a post-natal tonic. She could not stomach it. I was her favourite, her pet. I did not know it, and I don't think she made it too obvious to the others until later. But I can still see the pedal motor-car that I got for a birthday. It was bright green plywood with headlights and real mudguards, spoked wheels and leatherette seats. It gave all of us endless pleasure for years; but it was a rich boy's toy. And in Lee's of Dun Laoghaire she and I were shopping when I spotted a luxury model motor-launch which I had to have. She bought it for me there and then. It was neither Christmas nor birthday. I also got my first bicycle: it served for each of us in turn.

After my First Holy Communion in June 1936, Monty and I took the 45A bus. (It ran to Dublin from Bray then and up to the War). At Aston's Quay we went on a mystery tour. It was on a special G.S.R. coach, black and cream and more streamlined than anything I had ever seen. The tour brought us to Dunboyne, Co. Meath. It was a case of travelling hopefully.

Two little ditties of the day have stayed with me as reminders of the state of the world in the mid-1930s:

> Please keep off the grass
> And let the ladies pass:
> Here comes Gandhi
> Riding on his ass

and:

Will you come to Abyssinia, will you come?
Bring your own ammunition and your gun.
Mussolini will be there
And he'll fight you fair and square
Will you come to Abyssinia, will you come?

Children's parties, tea on the lawn, a maid called Doris (who got me to pee on the garden from an upstairs window: she thought it was hilarious to see my "tinny" as she called my penis); my brother's convalescence and my mischievous

Uncle Jack Cronin's Ford 10 De Luxe and my new toy complete with Cronin cousins, Margaret and Barbara, about 1936.

decision to pee in his glass of milk - these memories are vague. What is far from vague is the appendicitis that hit me early in 1937 and caused me such severe pain that I lay on my bed thumping my feet against the wall. Monty seemed reluctant to get the doctor, who was my uncle Jack Cronin, until my appendix burst and I was taken in Jack's Ford 10 De Luxe to Jervis Street Hospital. Mr. Arthur Chance was the surgeon and I spent a month there surrounded by little Dinky racing cars on a tray and a toy terrier given by Mr. Collis of Lee's Stores, a friend of my parents'.

What I only now realise is that Monty was seven months pregnant with Aedine, yet she journeyed to Dublin by bus every day for that month. Jim visited too, but that didn't seem to have the same importance for me. And when the big steel stitches were taken out and I could at last go home, my treat was a visit to the cinema to see "Captains Courageous" with young Freddie Bartholomew, the male equivalent of Shirley Temple.

CHAPTER 2

IRELAND TODAY

That year, 1937, brought a lot of change. Jim bought Florenceville a mile away for £850. Mrs Henry, a sister-in-law of Augustine Henry the botanist, had an almost exotic garden with shrubs and palm trees given to her by Augustine, and a walled orchard with thirty-four apple trees, and paths lined with box hedge. It had a large eucalyptus too, a tree that featured in family history in 1940. A children's paradise, with a small wood in its one and a half acres, and a real drive from the road, not as long as memory pictured it. Nor was the house as big.

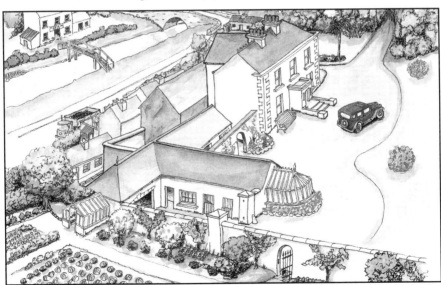

Florenceville reconstructed from memory by Gerry O Donovan 1992.

Florenceville, now called Millfield, was bound on the west by St. Rita's, on the north by Mill Lane, on the east by the Shankill-Ballybrack road, and on the south by Beechlands, then the home of Dr. William Roche, a well-known doctor in the district and head of Loughlinstown Hospital. Across the wall into Beechlands we could see the ruins of Shanganagh Castle in Dr. Roche's garden.

"Oh, no", says Canon Scott [1] in "The Stones of Bray", "it is not the place that is now called Shanganagh Castle on the Dublin Road. That is indeed also in the townland of Shanganagh, but on the southern border of it, whereas the old castle which Thomas Lawless built, and which afterwards was held, and probably enlarged, by the Walshes, is right on the northern boundary . . . One side of the keep of Shanganagh Castle is left, if we may use such grand terms of these old fortified houses . . ."

Dr. Ball [2] in his history of County Dublin says the castle was destroyed by fire in 1763. It was in the possession of the Roberts family by then. I have no recollection of having played in the ruins and can only assume that we were afraid of Dr. Roche.

Gerry got peritonitis about a year after I did, and he too survived and was treated to the cinema afterwards. I was sent to a new school, also private. St. Ann's in Dun Laoghaire was a happy place for me and I don't know to this day why I was taken out to go to the Presentation Brothers' School in Glasthule down the road. Presumably money.

St. Ann's - portly Mrs Russell and slim Miss Bath - seemed to be full of cousins. Deirdre was the daughter of Dan and Dorothy O'Donovan. Ruth Brennan, who had been with me in Bray, was the daughter of "Uncle" Joe Brennan, Jim's first cousin, then Chairman of the Currency Commission, possessor of a pale blue Packard and living in

And then there were four. Aedine was just born when this photograph of me and Sheila and Gerry was taken in 1937.

Crinken House on the Bray side of Shankill. Leon Ó Broin has written his life [3]. Deirdre and I were good friends right up to university and beyond. She and I played hockey with Ruth Brennan, Mary Lydon, Marie Cantwell, Mary Fleury,

Evanna McGilligan, Louis Nolan and Jerome Dowling - how many can I remember? "Me Tarzan. You Jane". The well-known Tarzan films of the 1930s were acted by Maureen O'Sullivan and Johnny Weissmuller. At St. Ann's we had two of Maureen O'Sullivan's sisters, Pat and Betty. The family lived at Saintbury by the sea at Killiney and the acting tradition is carried on by Maureen's daughter, Mia Farrow. The school was remarkable for the breadth of its curriculum. Certainly at nine I was learning the three Rs plus German - in the old Gothic script - presumably Irish, and geography. The German got me into trouble when Monty brought me down to Carraroe in Connemara

Eddie Toner on Killiney beach with my mother (left), me and Gerry.

where Todd Andrews and his wife Mary had a summer house. At lunch one day, Mary's mother, Mrs Coyle, asked for a second helping and young smart-ass could not help saying sotto voce: "Die gierige Grossmutter". I had not thought that the old lady spoke German. Red faces all around, but they were a tolerant family, including David and Niall, the politicians, who were my juniors.

Mary Andrews' brother was Donny (Donovan) Coyle, the West of Ireland businessman who gives me an excuse to mention yet another motor-car. He

The real Shanganagh Castle photographed by me in 1946

drove us back to Dublin in his Dagenham built Ford V-8 22 h.p., the most luxurious vehicle I had been in. (Jim in those years had a succession of 14.9 Fords, second hand. No social stigma then attached to buying second-hand cars any more than it did to renting flats or houses. The wonder was to have a car at all).

It was a busy and productive year for Jim. In June 1936 he had launched *IRELAND TO-DAY,* a brave periodical covering matters social, economic, political and cultural. This venture, in which his friend, Eddie Toner the co-founder of the Irish Film Society acted as business manager, was founded and edited by Jim, though because of his job in the public service, he could write in it only anonymously or pseudonymously. I write of *IRELAND TO-DAY* in hindsight. I knew little or nothing of it when I was eight or nine except driving with Jim to Dublin and being left in the car while he had meetings with people such as Frank Pakenham (Lord Longford). He would tell me who was at these meetings, but Longford's is the only name I recall.

I want to pay this posthumous tribute to Jim, so I intend shamelessly to plunder an article written in 1988 in *The Irish Times* by my friend Dr. Brian Kennedy of the Australian National Gallery. Calling *IRELAND TO-DAY* "an important example of courageous intellectual publishing", Kennedy wrote:

> The periodical survived for twenty-two monthly issues from June 1936 to March 1938. It was printed in Dublin using all-Irish materials and edited by James O'Donovan (1896-1979), an E.S.B. employee, who was a prominent figure in the Republican movement. Following the completion of his master's degree in chemistry at University College, Dublin, he became Director of Chemicals on the General Staff of the Irish Republican Army in the War of Independence. He was principal architect of the notorious S-Plan bombing campaign in Great Britain during the Second World War.
>
> It is important to establish Jim O'Donovan's editorship once and for all because an error perpetrated by Fr. Stephen Browne, S.J., in 1936, attributing the editorship of *IRELAND TO-DAY* to Michael O'Donovan (the writer, Frank O'Connor), has been repeated by many scholars and writers, most recently in the catalogue of an exhibition of Irish periodicals (1987).
>
> A man of wide interests and high intellectual calibre, with a fascinating circle of friends and associates, Jim O'Donovan brought together in *IRELAND TO-DAY* nearly all of the major writing talents of the 1930s in Ireland. The editorial committee included Sean O'Faolain (books), Owen Sheehy Skeffington (foreign affairs), Liam Ó Laoghaire (films), John Dowling (art), Éamonn Ó Gallchóbhair (music), Seán Ó Meadhra (theatre) and Edward Sheehy (succeeded O'Faolain as books editor).
>
> *IRELAND TO-DAY* was founded because of Jim O'Donovan's perception of the need, in Seamus Kelly's words, "for a magazine that would be the voice of advanced opinions on political, sociological, artistic, religious and international affairs". It aimed to establish itself as "the voice of all Ireland". Ten of its principal

contributors hailed from Belfast and seven of these were graduates or professors of Queen's University. The periodical was reviewed favourably in England and in America but Irish attitudes to its appearance were generally more cautious. The "leftist" tone of many of the articles was regarded with suspicion.

The leading writers in *IRELAND TO-DAY* were pro-Republican in the Spanish Civil War and viewed Franco as a reactionary dictator. In Dublin this was translated as pro-Communist and anti-Catholic. A whispering campaign began in Dublin targeted against *IRELAND TO-DAY*, particularly at Owen Sheehy Skeffington's articles on foreign affairs. A decision was made in March 1937 to drop Sheehy Skeffington but the financial damage had been done. The business manager, Edward Toner, found that the list of advertisers had dried up and although *IRELAND TO-DAY* survived for another twelve issues, its fate was sealed.

In fact there was no way a periodical like *IRELAND TO-DAY* could survive without major financial backing. Nevertheless, the periodical left a legacy of liberal thinking and a wealth of literary material which has not received due respect and attention.

The articles in *IRELAND TO-DAY* reveal that, during the 1930s, Auden's "low dishonest decade", there was a small core of high-minded and sincere idealists in Ireland who were anxious to break moulds and to establish new horizons. *IRELAND TO-DAY* spanned the exciting months of Spanish Civil War, the Blueshirt movement, and the preparations for and passing of the Irish Constitution.

It was topical and progressive and anybody who thinks that *THE CRANE BAG* (1977-85) was radically new would do well to look at *IRELAND TO-DAY*. Subjects such as national identity, censorship, Irish literature, film, drama, foreign policy, language, design in industry, were each featured and discussed with intelligence and constructive provocation. *IRELAND TO-DAY* was too strident for the Ireland of its day. Most people believed censorship to be a good idea but Sean Ó Faolain warned in *IRELAND TO-DAY*: "Our Censorship, in a word, foolishly squeamish, tries to keep the national mind in a state of perpetual adolescence . . . ." The index of contributors to *IRELAND TO-DAY* reveals a formidable array of talent. In many respects, *IRELAND TO-DAY* was the successor of *THE IRISH STATESMAN* and the predecessor of *THE BELL* in the history of Irish intellectual periodicals. Many of the contributors wrote for all three, others made their publishing debut in *IRELAND TO-DAY*. A sample list gives an idea of the quality - Brian Coffey, Thomas McGreevy, Frank O'Connor, Peadar O'Donnell, Sean O'Faolain, Michael Tierney, Lennox Robinson and Mervyn Wall.

While he has been mentioned often in histories of the War of Independence and about the "Emergency" years in Ireland, Jim O'Donovan was most proud of his work as editor of *IRELAND TO-DAY*. He died in 1979 without receiving the credit he deserved. It is timely that after fifty years the importance of *IRELAND TO-DAY* should be placed on record and its value as a historical source established beyond doubt.

Two things remain to be said about *IRELAND TO-DAY*. First, the confusion about the editorship has been carried on into Robert Welch's "Oxford Companion to Irish Literature"[4], published in 1996, sixty years after Father Browne's error. Secondly, the dropping of Owen Sheehy Skeffington was a shameful piece of expediency, brought on by panic at the drop in sales, which in turn was caused by clerical and lay Catholic pressure on business advertisers and on newsagents visited by people who suggested that they "take that red rag off their shelves", as Eddie Toner put it.

Although she could have been bitter about Jim's decision (and it was his, not his editorial board's, so Eddie Toner told me), Skeffington's widow Andrée in her biography of "Skeff"[5] lets my father down gently enough when she says:

. . . Pressure on the editor increased to the point of having the magazine boycotted in shops, and Owen was asked to write a valedictory note to his readers, which he did, observing: "There are some who do not feel safe to speak their opinions until all opposition has been silenced". It did not appear. There was no explanation and the editor never communicated with Owen again. He did, however, deposit Owen's note together with his files, in the National Library, adding the comment: "This is the production that finally decided me not to publish any announcement whatever as to Skeffington's leaving, but simply to appear without him". Captain John Lucy, author of "There's a Devil in the Drum"[6](one of the better books to come out of the Great War), took over the Foreign Commentary in *IRELAND TO-DAY* until its demise in March 1938. John Lucy, bewifed and bechildered as he says in a letter below, was the father of Seán Lucy, erstwhile professor of English at University College, Cork. I vaguely recall visiting him with my father at Glenageary House. I remember that Seán had a sister Kate and that the three of us played together. The letters I give below were a late discovery, found in John Lucy's book. They demonstrate both Lucy's delicious sense of humour and the seriousness with which he donned the mantle of Owen Sheehy Skeffington. And they show the money problems that my father encountered.

> Glenageary House,
> Glenageary,
> Co. Dublin.
> 26th Oct. 1937

The Editor,
Ireland Today,
(Babu Style)
Reminder No. 1

Sahib,
　　Your slave Lucifer, wielder of the sword, but a poor scribe in all senses craves to call your honourable attention to a slight lapse in your acountancy department to wit - no cheque to date for his despised effort of last month.
　　Being bewifed and bechildered this is bloody hard lines like to brother scribbler who asking for increment got excrement that is dejobbed.
　　Restrained by customs of caste system very strict, I have forbourne [sic] to approach you on bended knees heretofore, for request hereintofore now brought humbly to your respectful and dignified notice. Therefore levy, that is sotospeak ante up, and in double measure for last and November efforts combined to maintain zeal and the excellence of smoothish cooperation.
　　Thou art my father and my mother O Editor.
　　　　I have spoken,
　　　　　　I have,
　　　　　　　　I,
　　Thine despicable commentator on strange affairs, and of meetings of men of high order outside this land of holiness and scholastic attainments as is written in the holy books of sacred tradition.

(J.F. Lucy) B.A. Failed.

Dear Sirrah,

My war baby "There's a devil in the drum" will reach you for review in the course of the next two weeks.

It is scheduled for issue by Faber and Faber on 17th March.

Please be kind to it.

1.   The book is a simple account of what happened to two Irish boys (my brother and I), who insanely enlisted before the war, of what happened, to our comrades in battle, how they reacted, how they died, and what they said in great emergencies. Some gay and gallant men are portrayed, both troops and officers. I saw them both from the angle of the man who fought in the ranks from the first battle Mons, and as an officer too, because I was commissioned before being wounded in the tank battle of Cambrai.

There are also cruel and thoughtless things, as well as the inevitably humorous described with little or no comment.

At any rate an adventure, and a major one I think, which might have happened to any young Irishman looking for trouble, and told for the first time by an Irish soldier.

Be kind to it.

The name is "There's a devil in the drum".

2.   With regard to foreign commentary. Kindly note that I am now in touch with most of the important foreign consulates in Dublin, and that they have begun to send me their communiques, and other propaganda. With these it is hoped to be able to maintain a good middle course in future notes, and to avoid bias. I have found the "Guardian" slipping up lately.

Please send any of the usual magazines lately published, when you can spare them e.g. "International Affairs" "National Review" and the like.

Many thanks,
Yours faithfully,
John Lucy

I enclose David Cecil's opinion of it.

Rockbourne,
Fordingbridge
Hants.

Dear Sean O'Faolain

Thank you so much for that book. You are right: it is damned good.

What a relief to find a writer on the war who realised that war is - unfortunatley - a normal activity of man: and therefore treats it unselfconsciously and without all the wailings and vapourings of the intelligentsia war-book writers. —do not misunderstand me I am violently anti-war, but I think it is no use pretending it is a sort of inexplicable exception to the usual and natural? run of human existence.

Alas it is a recurrent and characteristic feature.
This recognition on John Lucy's part makes his book far more moving, and fills it with a real sense of tragedy.
Besides, how well he writes!

I thought the description of that sleep march a little masterpiece. He is so terse and so virile in his use of words and yet with none of the he-man affectations of the Hemingway school. I read the book straight through - neglecting my work, with absorbed interest and admiration both for its literary merits and for the author's character. Do tell him how very much I admired it.

(I hope we shall meet again so - - - The rest private)

Yours Ever,
(Sd) David Cecil.

The David Cecil referred to was Lord David Cecil, the English biographer of Melbourne, Cowper, Austen, and many more. He was thirty-six when he saw John Lucy's book. Because he belonged to the oldest and most aristocratic of British families, he had unique access to private papers. He was the youngest son of the fourth Marquess of Salisbury and married Rachel, the daughter of the critic and editor Desmond MacCarthy.

Jim owed money to the Wood Printing Works in Stafford (now Wolfe Tone) Street. To pay his debt he wrote to his distinguished contributors seeking their help in the form of an autographed book, which he could then sell. This scheme was so successful that the debt (about £150) was paid and there was a surplus of autographed books from which my brother and I benefited in the end.

In the late 1960s, a new enterprise was born - the reprinting of "little magazines" in bound facsimile editions. To the 200 or so British and American magazines that were so published, in Ireland the *Bell* and *Ireland To-day* were selected by David Kraus of the Kraus Reprint Co. of New York. My father at last made some money out of his creation.

CHAPTER 3

THE S-PLAN

Enter Seán Russell, Director of Munitions on the pre-Truce IRA staff and, like Jim, an anti-Treaty man in the Civil War (1922-23). In 1938, the leadership of the IRA was radically changed and Russell became Chief of Staff, replacing the more moderate Maurice ("Moss") Twomey and pursuing his dream of a bombing campaign against England. Somehow, I suspect by flattery, Russell enlisted the support of my father in this doom-laden enterprise. Jim was 42, had a wife and four children, a mortgage and a good job. Yet he was seduced into devising the S (for Sabotage)-Plan which was designed to hit the enemy, England, in her infrastructure.

"Tall, thin, with an accent more English than Irish, O'Donovan had graduated from University College, Dublin, in science", says Carolle Carter [7] of California. "He had lost three fingers of his right hand in an explosion during an early experiment . . . He never intended rejoining an organisation he did not feel was 'decent', but did agree to lend a hand because the IRA had no one qualified to discuss things on a high level, particularly with the Germans".

Reading that description of my father is painful to me. He was not tall and an American would not know an educated Irish accent when she heard it; but the sense of superiority displayed by Jim in his attitude to the IRA rings true. I would prefer that he had not spoken thus with Carter, but I am not surprised that he did. She saw him in Our Lady's Manor, Dalkey, in 1969.

James T. Farrell, [8] the American novelist met Jim, Moss Twomey, John Dowling and Andy Cooney in our house on 22 August, 1938. Next day, after a

The only family holiday that I recall was at Youghal in 1940.

long night in which he found the group "curiously insular and eccentric in their political attitudes", he noted in his diary: "O'Donovan is very quiet and shy, but probably the most intelligent of the lot".

Several visits by dark-hatted men in a green Morris Ten with "Dark Rosaleen" attached to its bonnet like the name of a house fixed on the front gate - chromed letters screwed on to a brown board - were linked in my mind with unexplained nocturnal excursions by my parents. After one of these nights, when I should have been asleep, I asked my mother: "Did your drive tonight have anything to do with the IRA?". She decided to tell me and said: "I might have known you would put two and two together".

Part of Jim's remit (he once told me that he had never taken a formal oath to the Republic) was to train young men like Brendan Behan how to make,

Maurice (Moss) Twomey talking to Aedine at her engagement party in 1967. Aedine is Mrs. Béla Sánta

handle and plant explosives. This work was carried on mainly by Paddy McGrath in Killiney Castle, then desolate, now the Fitzpatrick Castle Hotel, and in the Home Market, Liam Lucas's shop near the corner of Stephen's Green and Cuffe Street, Dublin.

Another aspect of Jim's commitment was to act as the IRA's liaison with the Abwehr, the German secret service headed by Admiral Canaris. This work involved three visits (February, April and August 1939), once bringing Monty as cover. These journeys, which were to seek German arms and radio equipment for the IRA, are well documented in Enno Stephan's book, "Spies in Ireland"[9]; Carolle J. Carter's "The Shamrock and the Swastika"[10] and Robert Fisk's "In Time of War"[11]. We children were not kept informed, though I found the key of my father's study and discovered the large radio transmitter (I recall the word superheterodyne was inscribed on it) on which a man came to make weekly transmissions in code to Germany. He was known to us as "Mister Saturday Night". A very long high aerial linked the house with a tree in the orchard. I have never understood why in the 1970s Jim did not take a libel action against Ladislas Farago [12] who in his book "The Game of the Foxes" wrote:

Dr. C.S. (Todd) Andrews at Aedine's engagement party held in 1967 at The O'Rahilly's house at Cursis Stream, Palmerstown. Todd is talking to my aunt Elgin, Madam O'Rahilly, and her son Michael, now The O'Rahilly.

In the meantime, two seemingly bona fide Irish revolutionaries reached Berlin to make their own deals with the Abwehr. One of them was Francis Stuart, a respectable scholar and noted author, who used to lecture at Berlin University on Irish literature before the war. The other was a certain "Held". His cover name was in the Abwehr's Central Registry, which described him, somewhat grandiosely and prematurely, as "our chief V-man in the Republic of Ireland". He was Jim O'Donovan, an elderly adventurer freelancing on the periphery of rebellion. He had nothing to do with the IRA except to use it as bait to ingratiate himself with the Abwehr and shake it down.

Mother at Florenceville, 1947.

Although Jim was interviewed by Stephan and Carter in the preparation of their books, I have no record of his being approached by Farago. At any rate, in spite of his pride (expressed later to me) in having been praised by the London *Morning Post* for the masterly strategy demonstrated in his S-Plan, Jim was in a very confused state of mind about his intervention and its dire consequences for his family. On the ideological side alone, he had been editor of a leftwing magazine and yet within a matter of months was collaborating with the National Socialist régime in Germany. He felt the contradiction of his position, though he would have cited in his own defence the Republican maxim that "England's difficulty is Ireland's opportunity".

He was sorry - he later said as much to me- for his decision to answer Seán Russell's call to arms. In later pages I quote what he said to a Republican commentator. But we never talked it out because there was a barrier of distrust between us that endured for much of his life. The distrust was not I am sure caused by his IRA connection: it was one of the results of my failure to like him and of what I saw from then on as his shabby treatment of my mother. Not physical abuse; more a lack of respect and caring for someone who soon had to shoulder a daunting burden of responsibility.

In January 1939, the IRA launched its offensive. An ultimatum was sent to the British Prime Minister, Neville Chamberlain; his Foreign Secretary Lord Halifax; the Northern Ireland Government; Adolf Hitler and Benito Mussolini, demanding a British withdrawal from the North within four days. The demand was sent in the name of "the Government of the Irish Republic". When nothing happened before the deadline was reached, "the people of all Ireland, at home and in exile" were summoned to compel the evacuation.

The violence began. A truncated form of the S-Plan caused explosions to damage factories; power stations and telephone exchanges in Britain on 16 January. Young men sent from Dublin or recruited in London pubs were arrested within a few days. Seán Russell's fond hope that casualties could be avoided was dashed when a bomb concealed under a manhole killed an innocent man in Manchester: another died in the left luggage office in a London station. After some 120 explosions had occurred, an old man and a schoolboy were among five killed in Coventry. This was on 25 August, six days before the Germans invaded Poland.

My father arrived home from his third German mission at the end of August, the sorry remnants of the S-Plan spattered across the front pages of the British newspapers. The Abwehr remained to be convinced of the credibility of the IRA and had given only moral support to the British campaign. And Hitler continued carefully to call de Valera Taoiseach.

A different voice raised on the merits of the S-Plan is that of John P. Duggan[13]. "The British", Duggan writes, ". . . were not so contemptuous [as the Germans] of the IRA capabilities. With the exception of the bungling, through panic, in Coventry the IRA bombing campaign . . . had been carried out with alarming efficiency. Their so-called S-Plan . . . was so efficiently prepared that MI5 thought it was the product of the Abwehr. It was in fact the brain-child of Jim O'Donovan, the ex-Clongowes science teacher. He subsequently derived amusement from the British supposition. He would not have given the Germans that much credit . . .".

Jim had taught science at Clongowes Wood College, but it was a brief post-graduation appointment held while the War of Independence was at its height in 1920-21. He commuted from Dublin to Sallins by motor-cycle.

The outbreak of war to me meant only excitement. The milkman from John Litton's Golden Ball Dairy called as usual that Sunday morning, 3 September 1939, and issued a dire prediction that this would be his last visit. It was not, of course, but as the war dragged on, butter, tea, sugar and bread, clothing, coal and petrol were rationed. Only essential motoring was allowed except for those equipped with one of two strange contraptions - a charcoal gas-producer fitted to the rear bumper and a huge gas bag fitted into a metal netting frame and fitted on the roof. My father got a 500-gallon drum of petrol and buried it in the garden.

One of the most popular wartime songs after "Roll Out the Barrel", "Run Rabbit Run" and "We'll Hang Out Our Washing on the Siegfried Line" - all British tunes - was "We're Saying Goodbye To Them All" of which part of the chorus was:

Bless de Valera and Seán MacEntee, they gave us black bread and a half ounce of tea.

"Black" bread was the grey batch bread made with soft Irish wheat, all our sources of hard wheat lying out of reach in France or Canada.

Still in pursuit of the arms and wireless equipment which he had sought during his pre-war visits to Abwehr II, Jim transmitted a radio message [14] on 8 October. The Abwehr, which generously if erroneously referred to Jim as "the chief agent in Ireland", commented that "his message gives no indication . . . . as to what supply route is now possible".

By this time, I was back in school, still with the Presentation Brothers but now in their college in Bray. I had been confirmed in St. Joseph's, Glasthule, in a ceremony of which I remember nothing except that when the bishop told the candidates to stand up and take the total abstinence pledge until we were 21, my mother told me to "sit down: you'll break it in a week". I do not know why she said so. Her snipe of Guinness was a thing of the past and while we sometimes had wine with a Sunday meal, I am not sure that I was even offered some. In view of my subsequent history, her command was however prophetic.

The wireless transmitter had been seized by the police, but not on our premises. It had been moved to the Brugha household. I wonder at the way Jim conducted such a risk-laden business while he held down a normal job, and offered no excuse for the Special Branch to pounce on him. Emergency legislation was passed by the Dáil as soon as the war began and a number of IRA suspects was interned at the Curragh Camp.

A custom had grown up by which Jim and Monty held a regular Sunday salon. I recall these evenings as occasions for general conversation on current affairs. The guests, often casual callers, were a mixed bag, not so much socially - they were certainly middle class - but in their political orientation. Professor Michael Tierney, a true-blue Fine Gael leader, would amicably fit with Moss Twomey; Todd Andrews of the Turf Development Board, a public servant of distinctly Fianna Fáil leanings, could be seen talking to his friend John Dowling, diehard Republican about to form a new party, Córas na Poblachta. And their equally vocal wives were there. Elgin and Mac (The) O'Rahilly and Dan and Dorothy O'Donovan represented the Barry and O'Donovan sides of the family.

This gathering may have been a deliberate ploy on my parents' part to place a mantle of respectability over the house. In his second book of autobiography[15], Todd Andrews waxes angry at Jim and his involvement in the S-Plan as "the most foolish and irresponsible act which bedevilled Anglo-Irish relations in my lifetime":

It was only many years afterwards that I learned of O'Donovan's connection with the bombing campaign, although he and his wife, a sister of Kevin Barry, were frequent visitors to our house and we to his.

I enjoyed those Sunday evenings, ignoring requests to go to bed until they became orders. School was a different matter. I made good friends, though I was soon to lose them. Jim Madden lived near the school; Brian and Noel Lawless in Shankill Castle, the Dooley brothers John and Paddy at Chantilly, a Department of Agriculture stud farm, and the de Portos, whose father Mariano was a Portuguese pioneer of our embryonic meteorological service. And John Duffy, in whose parents' sweet shop on the Vevay Road, I was allowed to serve. And Tony Drennan of the big grocery shop on the Main Street.

But the Brothers were fond of the cane and careless about whether it hit your hand or wrist. Brother Berchmans and Brother Snowy Lewis were hard men but not sadists like the aptly named Brother Angelo. Angelo's joy was to twist Tony Drennan's ear. I deeply felt the injustice of it.

Worst of all, I recall, was the Brothers' decision to break open the sealed box of Primary Certificate exam papers on Irish. They obviously felt that the school would be let down if we did not do well in Irish, so they let us see the papers beforehand.

CHAPTER 4

GOERTZ LANDS

In April 1940, I had to go to hospital again. I was told that some of the poison left over from my peritonitis of three years earlier had stayed in my system, so I spent a month in St. Joseph's Ward of Jervis Street Hospital under Sister Isidore. My memories were of unwelcome visits by Jim, who gave me "David Copperfield". I would not read it because it was his gift. Such a surly brat I was. A boy across the ward taught me the words of "The Boston Burglar" and told me of visits to "the Maro", the Mary Street Cinema near the hospital where you could gain admission by bringing a few jam jars. And then there was the night nurse. My treatment involved heat lamps every day, so I was quite red and sore under the guard designed to keep the blankets away from my body. Every night Nurse Eileen Horgan came with a bottle of soothing oil and gently stroked me all over. It was, though I did not know it, my first sexual experience, and I loved it and thank her for it. Leaba i measc na naomh go raibh aici.

On 9 April, 1940, Norway and Denmark were "offered the protection of the Reich" and on 10 May the German Army invaded Belgium and the Netherlands. The hospital was full of rumour and excitement. We realised that the *Sitzkrieg* was over and the *Blitzkrieg* had begun.

Five days before the invasion of Belgium, Dr. Hermann Goertz was dropped from a Heinkel 111 bomber near Ballivor, Co. Meath. His second parachute carrying a spade and his wireless set was lost. By asking two Meath men he found that he was 70 miles from his appointed meeting place. He had been told to contact Iseult Stuart, the wife of Francis Stuart the novelist. Stuart was then lecturing in Berlin and about to embark on his second career as a broadcaster on

*Dr. Hermann Goertz taken in 1946
after his release.*

the Irish Service of German Radio. Goertz's real aim was to meet Jim O'Donovan, still the Abwehr's "chief agent in Ireland". But to forestall arrest on his way to Florenceville, he was to seek Mrs. Stuart's aid first. She knew nothing of this plan.

Goertz marched by night to her remote house in Laragh, Co.Wicklow, avoiding policemen who guarded the River Boyne and discarding his uniform. "For the rest of my march I wore breeches, riding boots, pullover and a small black beret", [16] he later wrote. He carried a large amount of money in English and American notes and incredibly had not been told that sterling was legal tender in Ireland. He had a .32 FN automatic, fifty rounds in a box, and a strong parachute knife in a leather sheath with a silver tip. He also carried a large number of maps which caused him some pain as they chafed him through his pockets. He was hungry and exhausted when he arrived at Iseult Stuart's having eaten nothing for four days. He was fifty years old.

Goertz had a job convincing her that he was a German officer and a friend of her husband's, but she eventually believed him and went to Dublin to buy him a suit and presumably to talk to Jim.

After supper, a stranger arrived by car to take him to a place of safety. This was Jim, and the first place of safety was my vacant room. Thereafter Goertz stayed in the garage by night. By day he was hidden behind the eucalyptus tree. My mother secretly brought him his meals and he hid his code in the eaves of the stable. He stayed about eight days altogether and met the new Chief of Staff, Stephen Hayes, who will figure large later on.

Goertz's next safe house was Konstanz on the Templeogue Road. The owner was Stephen Held, an Irish-German industrialist, who had already been to Berlin to talk to the Abwehr. Goertz there had his second meeting with the

Bray c. 1941 as seen by me. Scraggs Garage is now Winston's. The ESB van never was.

Chief of Staff. Seán Russell had gone to America and Stephen Hayes had succeeded him. Goertz went around unarmed: he had given his automatic and his knife to Jim, who visited his German protégé almost daily.

I tell so much with hindsight because this long tale of espionage and intrigue, the subject of so many books, involved me and my future so directly.

In his biography of Frank Ryan[17], Sean Cronin baldly states that James O'Donovan's "politics were pro-German". He says that Stephen Hayes, the discredited Chief of Staff of the IRA, blamed the tenor of the broadcasts for the fact that the secret transmitter was seized "during a propaganda broadcast in Dublin in December, 1939". Some of the broadcasts were anti-Semitic, says Cronin. Hayes, claims Cronin, stated that "O'Donovan wrote the scripts and because of their anti-Jewish flavour, the Government was aware of 'German influence in our ranks' and was determined to silence them".

These are serious charges, and I have no documentary evidence to refute them. Left-wing Republicans such as George Gilmore were deeply disturbed by the possibility of an alliance with National Socialist Germany. In an interview

Bray Seafront c. 1941. The submarine and the seaplane did not exist. The anti-aircraft gun emplacement on the Head had by 1950 become the Holy Year cross that still stands.

with Seán Cronin in 1973, Gilmore said:[18] "Jim O'Donovan was the most Fascist-minded. We were in Mountjoy prison together in 1923 and he was anti-working class".

Stephen Hayes was arrested by the Northern Command Staff of the IRA in June, 1941. He was charged with "treachery and conspiracy to betray the Republic", court-martialled and imprisoned. He made a lengthy and detailed statement while he was in detention. The bones of this incredible document was that he had conspired with the Government, and specifically with Dr. Jim Ryan, Minister for Agriculture; Tom Derrig, Minister for Education; Senator Christy Byrne of Wicklow, and Larry de Lacy, a sub-editor on *The Irish Times* and a brother-in-law of Stephen Hayes, to, in its own words, "wreck the Irish Republican Army".

Was this tale of duplicity, murder and betrayal a farrago of nonsense? Or the truth? Or partly true? I read it first within a few years of its making because it was distributed by the IRA to all senior officers of the police and a friend at UCD was the son of a superintendent. I did not absorb its import then, or even link Hayes's "confession" to my father's arrest. Now I simply do not know.

Seán Cronin writes[19]:
How much reliance may be placed on Hayes's testimony written under sentence of death and obviously designed to buy time? Many of the details are wrong, of course, and Hayes wrote that Larry de Lacy drafted the ultimatum to Lord Halifax for the Army Council and was a member of the Department of Publicity with James O'Donovan, which Russell set up.

O'Donovan denied ever meeting de Lacy. "I would put little faith in what Stephen Hayes would say", O'Donovan said (in an interview at Our Lady's Manor, Dalkey, with Seán Cronin, 30 June , 1975)[20]. "But I was only nominally active. I did some work with Sean Russell and I have regretted it ever since". O'Donovan controlled communications, such as they were, with Germany. "It was foolish for me personally. It got me into the Curragh for two years. That was one part of my folly. I had to fight my employers for years afterwards to get back a few pence from the Electricity Supply Board". Communications with Germany mainly concerned trying to get Goertz back home in order "to disabuse them of any idea of the little common sense or practical assistance they could expect from the IRA".

Historians of the Republican movement differ on the validity of Stephen Hayes' "confession". Its effect on the morale of the IRA was devastating, some members believing its contents were convincing; more accepting that Hayes must have acted treacherously even if the details were sometimes confused and erroneous. Only a few knew exactly what had happened in Roger McHugh's cottage in Glencree and the two other places where Hayes was interrogated. And Seán McCaughey who presided over the court-martial, lay silent in Portlaoise where he died on hunger and thirst strike five years later.

For me, now, the salient fact is that the IRA's "Special Communiqué" containing Hayes's sworn testimony was issued on 10 September, 1941, the month in which my father was arrested and interned. The connection is clear.

I leave it to the reader to decide whether to believe that a man who made considerable sacrifices to launch and edit and write for a left-wing liberal magazine was likely within the next two years to write the scripts of anti-Semitic broadcasts.

In September 1941, just as my brother and I were setting off for school, eight Garda cars arrived at Florenceville. They were under the command of of Superintendent W.P. Quinn, who headed the Bray Police district, and Sergeant (later Commissioner) Michael Wymes. They arrested and interrogated Jim. They questioned Monty, our maid Mary Conroy from Clonaslee, Co. Laois, and the three of us (Aedine was only four and too young to tell anything of value). They searched the house and grounds, pulled books out of shelves, drawers out of desks and clothes and toys out of cupboards. There was paper everywhere. But they found nothing of consequence.

When they asked Mary Conroy about visitors to Florenceville, her reply was so convincing that it might have been rehearsed. The truth was that she knew nothing of strange men coming or going and rattled off the names of Michael Tierney, Eddie Toner, Todd Andrews and other upright citizens who had nothing to do with my father's other life.

So the security forces, whatever they had been told by their informants, could charge Jim with nothing. But they had the power to intern anybody without trial and they took him away, first to the Bridewell in Dublin, where their interrogation got rougher, and then to No. 1 Internment Camp on the Curragh of Kildare. He was back behind the wire again, a position he had last occupied before he was released in July 1924.

Jim had been jailed in most of the prisons and camps. His damaged right hand was his own doing, the result of an experiment conducted at the Bottle Tower in Churchtown which then lay in open fields. He had designed a hand-grenade and brought some senior IRA men to watch a demonstration. He threw the grenade into the open window of a derelict house and failed to withdraw his hand in time. Soon after that he was arrested by the British and because his hand was severely wounded was taken to the Drogheda Memorial Hospital on the Curragh. The doctors wanted to amputate but he talked them out of it and this saved his hand so that all his life, through he greeted people with his left, he could use a pen to great effect. Periodically, pieces of grenade would surface but apart from embarrassment he suffered no ill effects.

How much he suffered in other ways in those places of incarceration I did not know until I got from Seán O'Mahony, that fount of knowledge on things

Republican, a poem that my father wrote in Arbour Hill on 25 September 1923. That date, it should be noted, was five months after the Civil war ended. The poem is subscribed: "Written on the fourth day of *absolute* and solitary confinement to cell", and is entitled "Quid Retribuam ......?"

"Quid retribuam Domino pro omnibus quae retribuit mihi? Calicem salutaris accipiam, et nomen Domini invocabo: laudans, invocabo Dominum, et ab inimicis meis salvus ero".

> Say what, O Lord, shall I return:
> Who have but deserved of thee
> That I should rue and writhe and burn -
> Foul in Hell's eternity.
> > Invocabo Dominum

> And not content O Lord with this
> Holding back dire penalty
> My soul hast Thou infused with bliss
> Soul that dredged in frailty!
> > Invocabo Dominum

> I've drunk, O Lord, of earthly wine;
> Loved; and scrupled not to be
> An outcast 'yond the pale of Thine
> All-availing charity.
> > Invocabo Dominum

> But come I now, O Lord, to taste
> Sweetnesses, unworthily —
> Salvation from Thy Chalice chaste:
> Praising, while invoking Thee.
> > Invocabo Dominum

> When guilt invites, O Lord, or when
> Hostile arms are choking me,
> Thy present shielding Love will then
> Summon to invoking Thee.
> > Invocabo Dominum

The title and quotation are from the pre-Conciliar Ordinary of the Mass.

In my missal An Leabhar Aifrinn (1952), the Latin is as my father has it, preceded by: Sul a n-ólann sé an Chailís deir sé. Beside the Latin is the Irish of An t-Ath. Benedichtus, O.C.D., printed in the old Irish type in Dublin and published by Oifig an tSoláthair, the Government Stationery Office. The missal was new when Jim gave it to me.

The words, from Psalm 115, verses 12 and 13, are: What shall I render to the Lord for all the things that he has rendered to me? I will take the chalice of salvation and I will call upon the name of the Lord. Praising, I shall call upon the Lord, and from my enemies I shall be saved.

CHAPTER 5

ROCK BOYS ARE WE

L ife in the Curragh was so appalling that some of the prison huts were set on fire in protest. That was on 14 December 1940, nine months before Jim arrived. The Army who controlled the camp "reacted immediately and harshly", as J. Bowyer Bell [21] tells us graphically:

> The camp was surrounded by fully armed soldiers backed by armoured cars. All the prisoners were rounded up by soldiers carrying small arms and locked into the remaining huts from Saturday evening to Monday morning without food. The suspected ring-leaders were taken out and forced to run through a double line of

Blackrock College, Dublin. An unpublished sketch by Raymond McGrath, P.R.H.A. The college has his watercolour of the Castle, part of the college. Done in 1941.

soldiers equipped with batons and revolvers. Most arrived at the other end bruised and beaten. They were then taken to the Glasshouse [the punishment block]. Some were beaten again and all kept in solitary confinement for ten weeks. On Monday morning when the rest of the prisoners were finally released from their huts, the soldiers were waiting outside with arms at the ready. When the men, as was the custom, began to line up in hut order for breakfast, the soldiers opened fire without warning. Apparently they had been informed that the prisoners would not be allowed to line up, but whatever the explanation they continued firing into the stunned and milling crowd. Barney Casey fell to the ground, shot in the back. A bullet grazed Martin Staunton's face and another struck Walter Mitchell's shoe bruising his heel. Bob Flanagan and Art Moynihan were hit. Then in the sudden silence Billy Mulligan walked directly to the gate and demanded a stretcher for Casey who was lying crumpled on the ground, his face and chest covered with a bloody froth. He died two hours later. To the prisoners then and later the massacre of 16 December was unprovoked and inexcusable, an exercise in brutality hushed up by the Government. At thesubsequent inquest Seán MacBride was allowed to ask a single question - "Why was Barney Casey shot in the back?" The inquest was adjourned . . . .

After the camp had settled down to an eternity of boredom and waiting, divisions among the 500 internees multiplied. Neil Gould Verschoyle, a dedicated Communist who had studied in Moscow and married a Russian, attracted those of leftist tendencies and repelled those devout Catholic men who demanded that he be ostracised. Jim was several times wakened in the night, told to get dressed and ready for release and taken to the Glasshouse to "sign the paper" proving his loyalty to the State. The inevitable result of his refusal was a beating and return to the hut. While Harry White [22] was there, Jim got him involved in an elaborate break-out which depended on the perimeter lights being cut. It failed.

The usual activities of prisoners flourished. A paper called *Barbed Wire* was started; classes in Russian were held by Gould; in German by Jim; in English and drama by Roger McHugh; in Irish by Máirtín ÓCadhain; football, chess and shows and dramas were played.

Monty was allowed to visit every month. She usually took Eddie Toner along for company on the two-bus journey which took all day. Jim passed messages to her. Written on cigarette papers, they were sometimes concealed in a piece of handicraft such as a holy picture in an embroidered frame. I remember one of those and the excitement of extracting the folded sheets. I was not allowed to read the contents.

But how did she manage? She was left with a house full of children, all the normal bills to pay, a maid and school fees to be kept up. I think she tackled the school question first. My brother Gerry and I were taken from the Presentation College in Bray and in the winter of 1941-42 dumped into Blackrock College as boarders. (Gerry began in Willow Park, the junior school).

For twenty years or more I lived under the misapprehension that our school fees were paid by our uncle Dan, who then was County Commissioner for Dublin, the County Council having been suspended for stated misbehaviour. Only then did I discover that Dan, an ex-pupil, had arranged with Dr. John Charles McQuaid, Archbishop of Dublin and ex-President of Blackrock, to get us into Blackrock. So no fees were paid. To the eternal credit of the Holy Ghost Fathers, no reference was ever made to the fact that we were virtual orphans; nor were we made to feel in any way different from the country shopkeepers' sons who made up the bulk of the boarders.

I was never the youngest in any class. I had been a sickly child and was among the older lads in my year. To that fact was added a decision to make me repeat the Intermediate Certificate exam in the hope of my getting a scholarship. I didn't get the scholarship, so I was told by Father Anthony Hampson, the Dean of Studies, that I had to cover the Leaving Certificate course in one year instead of two. So I skipped Fifth Year, but was denied the privileges that attached to Sixth Year life in "The Castle": better food, smoking time, a cubicle of my own. So it was classes in the Castle and study and sleep in the main college building. And no explanation. Anyway I got five honours in the Leaving, so hump the begrudgers.

To get an education for Sheila was not so easy. She had bad asthma and was regarded, she says, as a nuisance by Monty. Her free schooling was arranged by Mother Ignatius of the Loreto Convent in Bray. Ignatius was an unusual and kindly woman, the mother of two Republican sons before she entered the order. Sheila's personal hell was in that school, but it was not her sponsor's fault and it does not belong to this story.

What does belong to this story is Sheila's memory of "the time de Valera had Jim taken out of jail to ask him if he'd be State Chemist. When Jim refused, Dev asked him to nominate someone else, which he did and was promptly sent back to jail". I have no recollection of that incident, but I do know that the Chief State Chemist appointed about that time was Bert (Hubert) Earle, the best friend of Todd Andrews.

Monty still had to live, so she took in what she called "P.G.s", paying guests. Miss Harrington and Mr. Hand were a peculiar couple whom I never got to know. I do not even remember the sleeping arrangements except that on holidays I had a bed elsewhere in the house. The guests - Miss Harrington was Mr. Hand's ward - had their own living room, cooked in the big kitchen downstairs and tended their allocated patch of the garden.

More adventurously, Monty set up a cottage cheese industry in partnership with the Attorney-General's wife. Kevin Dixon was the A.G. (later a High Court judge), a member of the well-known family that included Dr. Eileen Dixon, the "Radio Doctor". Their father Martin was a builder in Dalkey and had, as it happened, done some work on Florenceville - a buttress in yellow brick dated 1911 and the art noveau mantelpiece in the drawing room testify to his skill. Kevin Dixon's wife Agnes and Monty started Roland Cheeses (called after the Dixons' son) in Violet Hill, Ballybrack. The cheese sold in what would now be termed delicatessens. Then they were the middle-class grocery shops such as Sewells and Findlaters.

It was a huge undertaking, running Florenceville, cycling to Violet Hill, making the cheese, then delivering it to Dublin, by bus, I suppose. When that time of year came around again, she also had to catch a tram from Dún Laoghaire to Blackrock to hear and see her son (me) perform in one of the annual Gilbert and Sullivan operettas.

Monty must have got some satisfaction out of having her own money. She complained to me that, while Jim took the only legacy (£200) she was ever left in order to prop up his City Chemical and Colour Company, which failed before I was born, he never let her have an allowance that she could dispose of herself. Perhaps there was a corresponding resentment when he was released and she had to hand back the reins of management .

The operetta brings me to sex. I think my first experience apart from Nurse Horgan, was when I was in the chorus of "Iolanthe", waiting in the wings and feeling the hand of a senior boy creep up my leg. He groped between my legs for a while. I did not have an erection: neither did I scream or object. That was it, short and not unpleasant, though quite incomprehensible to me.

Later there was a little bed-hopping in the dormitory of 60 boys (and one turf fire); a double hotel bed with a best friend during a holiday in the country, where I think I was the initiator of some groping, and a one-sided (on his part) love affair with an older boy which involved cycle rides during the holidays to the pier at Dún Laoghaire. It all sounds pretty harmless now, but I can recall a deep penetrating sense of guilt and once after an ejaculation the forlorn feeling as I later lay in the bath at home that I was pregnant. How was I to know? The priests frightened the bejasus out of us with homilies on not looking down when we were having a pee; but they did not say why. Thank God for books and dictionaries and smutty jokes. When Jim was released he eventually got around to talking about the birds and the goddamn bees while we paced Carrigolligan mountain, both of us so uncomfortable that I had to tell him that he was just a few years late.

Relations between my father and myself were strained. I wrote at the time: "He thinks I lack the reverence due to him as my father, thinks - God only knows what he thinks - perhaps he blames my mother. On my part, I think he is unreasonable very often, too often, but I realise, and am sorry, that this is not sufficient explanation of my unnatural and unfilial attitude towards him. Sometimes he gets sarcastic: 'I'm just the bread-winner, the guy that provides the dough'. From this bitterness he veers to a mood that seems to cry out for love and affection; not being demonstrative or emotional by nature, and being a very bad actor, I can't respond. There are even times, but they're getting more seldom, when we are on quite good terms and go for a walk, while he tells me all about his work".

To balance my negative view of my father, I strongly feel that I should insert an outside observer's view of Jim and Monty. In 1987, Dr. Brian Kennedy wrote me a long letter about his discoveries. He had been going through Jim's papers, long lying in The O'Rahilly's garage at Cursis Stream and then languishing in mine. (When Brian had put some order on them, I gave them to the archive in University College, Dublin, not knowing that Jim had donated what he saw as valuable to the National Library. So the scholar who wants to research his life will have to journey between two institutions). Brian wrote:

A facet of your father which might surprise you is his extremely tender relationship with your mother. She was an incredibly loyal and tough lady who loved her husband dearly. It is a funny thing but I don't think we are ever fully aware of our parents as lovers . . . .

I am grateful to Brian for his invaluable insight. And to the testimony of my good friend Louis McRedmond, who offers this view:

When we (Louis and Maeve) were in Rathgar, your father and mother used to invite us in for a cup of tea/coffee if we met on the way home after Sunday Mass. Their friendliness, interest in our doings and tolerance of our Michael - a toddler at the time - remains in my memory, and I recall them as a kindly, rather old-world couple, courteously warmhearted and seemingly settled in their ways. I liked them very much.

Monty managed. Not only the house, the business, the P.G.s and the children, but the persistent illness of one of them. Sheila's asthma got no better. Father Alfred ("Alfie") Chamberlain, the new Dean of Discipline, and John Gannon, a teacher cleric who tried to impart English to me even when I told him that persuade was not spelt pursuade, both tried to help Sheila in their ways, one being hypnosis.

What I picked up from Father Chamberlain was the way not to handle teenagers. It was bad enough when he tried to censor the cowboy movies in the school hall by putting his hand over the lens just when he thought the man was about to kiss the girl. It was his obsession with table manners that I remember. In his Sunday morning allocutions he made it perfectly clear that if your parents had not already taught you how to use a knife and fork, there was nothing he or the college could do for you. He was very class conscious.

Class was not discussed at school, not even by the B.V.P. Society (Bonum, Verum, Pulchrum) initiated by Father John Chisholm in my time. But there were four types of boy. In descending social order, there were the dayboys who lived in the area, had "normal" families and took not a blind bit of notice of the rest of us. (Though I made a few good friends among them, friends I could see during holidays because I lived less than ten miles away). There were the rich boarders, distinguished by the size and variety of the parcels they got from home and more importantly by the fact that they were served "extras" - bacon, egg and sausage - for breakfast. This in the middle of a world war. There were the ordinary boarders like myself who for five years poured the Carigeen moss pudding into the inedible soup at dinnertime and otherwise lived off porridge, bread, a "print" of butter and tea. We tended to share our parcels from home. Last there were the scholastics, the boys who were getting a free education in the expectation that they would become priests. They had to wear a soutane - black, down to their ankles - all the time; had separate dormitories, refectory and play areas and were despised by all. I became friendly with one of them. He was from the West of Ireland and he abandoned his religious studies, went to university and became the successful manager of a semi-State company.

By Father John ("Dryballs") Ryan I was first introduced to journalism. He suggested that I contribute to the *Blackrock College Annual*, and I enjoyed writing those pastiches of the year's activities as well as I did writing the words of a hymn to Our Lady of Fatima for Father Joe Corless, the musical director of the choir. My self-confidence was growing with these and academic attainments, and I even became a sort of joiner - of the B.V.P., the St. Vincent de Paul Society and the Legion of Mary. I think now of how innocent and silly we must have looked to the poor boys convalescing in Linden Home and the sailors of the merchant ships tied up at Dublin docks when we presented ourselves with our little parcels and our divine message of hope on a Sunday morning.

In my sporadic diary for 1946 I wrote:
There was one fellow there who told me he lived in Kevin Street; (that, as far as I know, is a street of the worst kind of rickety slums). He asked me did I go to dances: I said I did, and he asked what dance-hall I went to, was it the Balalaika? I felt a kind of pity for one whose life was lived in an environment where the Balalaika (a vulgar dance-hall in the city) represented the star to which to hitch one's chariot . . . .

No comment. How about this one?

Every Sunday, the President of the College invites seven fellows to dinner, so that he can get to know them intimately. I'm afraid the idea is a flop, because his bearing is not such as would promote confidences or even intelligent conversation. Besides, the parties are badly picked; I was not particularly attached to any of those invited, nor they to one another or to me. The President monopolised the conversation and kept it almost constantly on the subject of art. Only three of us did any talking, myself, my pet aversion, and a casual friend of mine.

No, it was not a success, at least yesterday.

Rugby for me was a lost cause. Blackrock was the best rugby college in the country, but I was puny, untrained and timid. To console people like me, there was the "Galaxy", an attempt by the manly fathers to give some credit to the swats. Rugby happened every Wednesday: the Galaxy members were given their treat once a year. The only one I recall was a train trip to Bray and a picnic in the Carlisle Grounds there. Talk about coals to Newcastle!

One day in 1943, my brother and I were summoned to the President's parlour. Inside was Jim, our imprisoned father, and we both made the drastic error of assuming that he had been released and was in turn releasing us. It turned out that Jim's sister, our Aunt Marguerite, had died and he was on parole for the day. Marguerite was the superior of St. Joseph's Orphanage in Dún Laoghaire. She had tried to teach me my tables while I was at St. Ann's and I could recall interminable sunny afternoons in the garden at Tivoli Road. But now I was not thinking of the dead aunt I scarcely knew, but looking at the reality that nothing had changed. I felt I had been tantalised and I got no joy from that parental visit.

On 30 April 1946, I wrote to my father a letter which began:

Dear Daddy, what does it feel like to be 20 years married? I suppose, though, that your wedding didn't involve such excitement and soul-searching as the same event would for a man younger and less used to excitement and thrills than you were. Still, it's a big - the biggest -adventure, and the fact that you were already a man of action must have helped you . . .

I hope I wasn't taking the piss out of him. He didn't think so at any rate. He preserved this and half a dozen other letters in his papers. I wrote to my mother - "Dear Mammy": (soon she was to ask us to call her mother) on the same day saying: "If I had successfully raised four children, I would be proud". So I must have meant it.

Another letter from me to my mother puzzled me for a long time while I was writing these memoirs. I couldn't talk about it until I solved its mystery.

On 30 January 1943, my fifteenth birthday, I thanked her for my birthday parcel, a jumper, a cake, and six oranges, four of which had been taken before I got the parcel. I merely reported the facts and expressed my thanks.

But think of it. Look again at the date. Where in the name of God did the oranges come from? Nobody in Northern Europe had seen an orange for years while the greatest war in history was being waged. Yet there I was, quite blasé about the loss of four of these exotic fruits.

It was my cousin Diarmuid, who lives in Boyle, Co. Roscommon, that suggested the solution. His father, Colman O'Donovan, had a year before been despatched by the Department of External Affairs to Lisbon, there to open an Irish diplomatic mission. It was a difficult task. He was being sent without staff to another neutral, Portugal, where no legation existed. He and his wife Moll (his first cousin) and their daughter Maureen took a flying boat from Foynes and set up house in a strange country whose language none of them then knew. He had fallen foul of the legendary Secretary of the Department, Joe Walshe, and this, I believe was his punishment.

At any rate, the decent Colman must have sent us a box of oranges grown perhaps in neighbouring and equally neutral Spain.

CHAPTER 6

WET BATTERIES

My summer holidays were special. A couple of summers I spent in Carlow, invited by Superintendent Jack Feore and his kind wife Mona to stay with my best friend Dermot Feore at Belmont, a vast house on the Kilkenny Road. We went from there to the Grand Hotel, Tramore, and enjoyed the pleasures of a splendid seaside resort. And of course we travelled by motor-car, courtesy of the State. It is a curious and perhaps Irish thing that while the father was a guest of the nation in one sense, the mother was working with the Attorney-General's wife and the son was staying with a senior policeman's family.

Part of most summers was spent with my aunt Shel, another sister of Kevin Barry's. At first her husband Bapty Maher was part of this household, a farmstead called Clogorrow three miles from Athy. Then the couple separated and Bapty retreated to his pub, grocery and undertaking business at 23 Leinster Street, Athy. Shel was good company, as were her five children. She had a sharp tongue and could be very funny so long as I was not the target. One summer, she invited my cousin Paddy Moloney to stay. My cousin Johnny and I did not like Paddy, so we thought of a mean trick to play on him. There was a large manure heap in the yard, more or less flat on top. We dug a hole about three feet deep in the manure, put sticks across the hole, covered the result with manure and then went looking for Paddy. We enticed him up on the heap, walked one on either side of him and watched as he fell into the hole. We got a good cruel laugh out of his misery and dirt, and we awaited events. Paddy at once wrote to his mother, who told him to come home immediately. Unfortunately my aunt Shel had to read the letter for Paddy and got the benefit of Aunt Kitby's comments on her and her other charges. Paddy went home to Dublin on the next bus.

There was no electricity at Clogorrow. The wireless worked on wet batteries that had to be taken to town by cycle or donkey and trap to be recharged. We used paraffin lamps in the bedrooms and in the main rooms, with a paraffin cooker in the kitchen. Breakfast was fried brown bread and tea, and if we were taking turf out of Kilberry bog or picking peas for Batchelors factory on Bapty's land, we took a packed lunch of batch bread lettuce and tomato sandwiches smothered in salad cream and washed down with Irel chicory "coffee". The tractor, the donkey and trap and the haybogey or slide were mere added attractions. To draw the turf out of the bog we used primitive carts, narrow and fitted with solid wooden wheels about 18 inches long and four inches thick. They were pulled by donkeys or ponies and I learnt that if the animal fell into a drain crossing a bridge, a donkey would lie patiently in the water but a pony would break its heart trying to get up.

Puberty brought only mild fun. Johnny and I made several trips to the outskirts of town, hoping to catch courting couples - doing what, we were not sure, though Johnny was more advanced than I. A crude joke of Johnny's concerned a Land Girl. (A quaint English custom in wartime was to make city girls replace the agricultural lads who had gone to war). This girl was told by the farmer to bring the cow to the bull. "Well", said the farmer when she returned, "how did you get on?". "Tophole", she replied. "Christ", he said, "I might have known you'd make a balls of it".

A great privilege granted to Gerry and me while we were at Blackrock was a weekly exeat. An exeat was permission to leave the college and we were allowed to go on Saturday afternoon until Sunday night. The reasons I suppose were that we were living within an ass's roar of the school and that our mother was alone. I have a vivid memory of returning to the college by tram at seven or eight on a dark winter's night, clutching my bag of unwanted sausage rolls and deeply dreading the lonely night ahead of me.

I think Monty needed us. She must have felt her isolation. She certainly made us welcome and we ingested her food and gossip with gusto. If there was news of Jim so much the better, but he was not a bad correspondent with us at school, though he had to keep within the limits that the camp censor imposed. An irony was that while he was in the Curragh he was awarded a bronze "Black and Tan" medal for his part in the War of Independence twenty years before. It was addressed to him at No. 1 Internment Camp, The Curragh.

School was the gulag. Real life was around Shanganagh. A friendship grew up between us children and the family of Michael and Eibhlin Tierney. Jim and the professor were old friends. He held the chair of Greek at University College, Dublin: she was a daughter of Eoin MacNeill, the Irish scholar who led the Irish Volunteers until he tried to countermand the order that precipitated the 1916 Rising. Una, the eldest Tierney, was of Garret FitzGerald's generation at a time when two years represented a generation. But Brídín, the next, and Michael, Niall and Martin were our playmates. The twins Myles and Denis were regarded as too young by us.

The Tierneys lived at Kilnamona, a fairly big house on the way to Shankill, now a retirement home. Opposite them were the Downeys of Rest Harrow, another large family and - a rarity of the time - possessors of his-and-her motor-cars. Mrs Downey owned one of the early Topolinos, a Fiat 500 with a manual windscreen wiper. Blaise and St. Clair were our friends. Mark already was in the Royal Air Force, a distant hero in our eyes, especially when he was literally shot down in flames and had to have much skin grafting done. He later married my cousin Maeve Brennan, sister of my contemporary Ruth. Gay, an architect , is still a friend and neighbour of Ruth's.

There were other families who had children of our age - the O'Neills, the Walshes, Rowans the seed merchants, the Dillons (Professor Theo Dillon was a brother of James the politician and one of the few orators in Dáil Éireann). Their houses were dotted from Killiney to Crinken, and they were nearly all Catholic middle-class people who went to Mass at St. Ann's Church in Shankill, a chapel of ease where the pastor was Father Tom Grogan. A painter and an unusually liberal thinker, Father Grogan was the only priest, to my recollection, to darken our door. Jim and Monty were God fearing people but they did not have any time for clerics. The institutional church had dirtied its bib in the eyes of many Republicans because of its threats of ex-communication against the anti-Treaty forces in 1922-23. For me, class ruled St. Ann's Church, where we sat in the front section for 6d.; the working-class people sat behind us for 3d.; and the hangers on at the back stood and were supposed to pay 1d.

When Jim was released in the spring of 1944, I remember being taken for a celebratory drink in a pub in Fleet Street. My grandmother, Kevin Barry's mother, lived in No. 8 Fleet Street, where all her children were born. The house served as a city centre meeting place for all her family. It was there, in 1937, that her cook Kate Kinsella called me "a little old man cut short". That was the year of the greedy grandmother, so you can see a pattern forming.

Kate Kinsella died that year at 84. A native of Ringsend, she was born in 1853 and joined the Barry family in 1879. She was the youngest of her large family and could recall the story of her mother carrying an infant in her arms outside the Richmond Penitentiary when Daniel O'Connell the Liberator was released, sick in mind and body, after his trial and conviction for conspiracy in 1844.

Kate herself was a friend of Tim Kelly, one of the Invincibles who killed Lord Frederick Cavendish, Chief Secretary for Ireland, and Thomas Henry Burke, Under Secretary, in what became known as "the Phoenix Park Murders" of 1882. One of the many gifts that graced that memorious woman was a genius for mental arithmetic. Her remarkable part in the Civil War is told in my "Kevin Barry and His Time". [23]

I was nine when Kate died. I write so much of her because I treasure her as a link with another age. My past is not a different country.

Jim was lucky. Because he had not been convicted of any crime, his employers, the Electricity Supply Board, willingly took him on again. But he did have, as he told Seán Cronin, a fierce struggle to get what he saw as his rights. I suppose he sought some kind of compensation or restoration of status or promotion due. I only know that he had to fight long and hard to get the position of Statute and Wayleaves Officer, a job that placed him in the department of the Secretary of the Board, his friend John Donovan. His brief was, I think, to enable the ESB to plant pylons and poles over land whose owners objected. I remember his joy when he won a case involving Lady Oranmore and Browne of Luggala. And his pride when he was proved right in a report on the future demand for electric current. His report predicted an annual growth of 10 per cent. He was laughed at by his colleagues until the forecast began to vindicate his judgment. It was the beginning of rural electrification.

CHAPTER 7

THE ROARING FORTIES

I was the only member of my family to go to university, a privilege granted only to those whose parents could afford the fees (Gerry and Aedine went to the National College of Art). There was no points system; there were few scholarships. Elitism ruled the roost. I am truly grateful for those three years in Earlsfort Terrace. I did not work hard and I did not get a good degree. There was an expectation that I would go on to become a third secretary in the Department of External Affairs, where my Uncle Colman served as minister or ambassador in several countries; but I was far too engrossed in college societies, the Students Representative Council, the *National Student,* dancing, women and above all drink.

It was the ideal life for an 18 year old and I embraced it with the abandon of a prisoner set free. I joined the Literary and Historical Society, the Law Society, the English Literature Society. I wrote for the *National Student,* helped to organise Rag Day, ran the Law and Commerce Dance with Frank Kelly, and was elected to the Students' Council. Frank Kelly, who later became temporarily engaged to my sister Sheila, added to my life skills by instructing me (in Jammet's Restaurant) on the joys of under-done fillet steak - the norm was the countryman's leathery T-bone - and by ridiculing my wearing a waistcoat with a single breasted dinner jacket. He was a son of Clem Kelly, a retail draper and member of my uncle Dan's inner circle, of which more. Frank went on to great things in the British and Australian tourist boards.

The degree I was aiming for was a B.A. in Legal and Political Science, a choice of course on which Jim consulted Michael Tierney. Politics was taught by

Canon O'Keeffe (there was quite a number of priests on the college staff; and there was a pervasive smell of Fine Gael everywhere). Canon O'Keeffe was the creator (as far as I know) of the dictum that a university is a place where sham pearls are thrown before real swine. The pearls included some very mediocre lecturers, but there were exceptions such as Paddy McGilligan, our Professor of Constitutional Law. McGilligan had been a distinguished Minister in the Cumann na nGaedheal Government of 1922-32 and was responsible for promoting the Shannon Scheme which electrified the country. His pet hate was the 1937 Constitution and by extension its principal author, Éamon de Valera. My college copy of Bunreacht na h-Éireann is grangerised out of recognition by comments ironic and sarcastic made by that brilliant man.

McGilligan had contested the auditorship of the L&H in 1910. I had no such pretensions, but I was a member of the committee in 1948-49 during the auditorship of Paddy O'Kelly who became a leading cancer specialist in the United States and died in New York in 1996. My future wife Karin O'Sullivan was on that committee and on Paddy Connolly's the year after. My cousin Deirdre was on that committee too. Desmond Fennell the writer served on O'Kelly's committee with me. The inaugural address was on "Quicksands of Peace". The speakers were Seán MacBride, then Minister for External Affairs; Colonel Crosthwaite Eyre, M.P., Señor Salvador de Madariaga the eminent writer and diplomat, and Senator Denis Ireland. I remember that one of us telephoned Áras an Uachtaráin to see whether President O'Kelly would like to receive de Madariaga. The reply was a frozen " *Who*?"

The Republic of Ireland was declared by the Inter-Party Government which had toppled Fianna Fáil in February. Political tensions ran high in the college and it became clear that, whatever the complexion of the UCD staff, there was a vocal streak of separatism and anti-British feeling in the L&H.

The historian Oliver MacDonagh served on Éamonn Walsh's committee in 1945-46 and ten years later was to write[24]:

. . . it is, I think, not unfair

Dr. Michael Tierney photographed by me at his new house, Westfield Park, Harold's Cross, in 1946.

to say that in oratorical merit and administration the L&H inclined towards Fine Gael; that in collective sentiment it was pro-Government [Fianna Fáil]; and that in collective voice and vote it was usually in opposition to the Government and often (particularly on issues such as Roger McHugh's internment) positively Republican.

Roger McHugh, who tutored me in English in my first year, was a friend of my parents and had, by dint of lending his cottage in Glencree so that the IRA could interrogate Stephen Hayes in peace and quiet, been interned with Jim on the Curragh.

Oliver MacDonagh says he was never a successful speaker. Neither was I. I always thought that drinking a number of pints would give me courage. It did no such thing. I was a social success and I should have left it at that. But I did not, and I made the alcoholic's mistake of doing the same thing time after time and expecting different results. That way lies madness.

I became auditor of the English Literature Society in 1948-49 and delivered my paper on "Censorship" to a crowd that was perhaps not as big as the L&H could muster on a good night, but was definitely outside my capacity to handle. To bolster my courage, I thought of a neat trick. Before the meeting I emptied the speakers' water-jug and filled it with gin for myself. I totally ignored the obvious risk that another speaker would need to wet his whistle. I can still see John Dowling's face as he tasted the contents of his glass. Before the meeting was organised, I had to submit my paper on censorship to the censor - the new President of the College, Michael Tierney, who had a heavy hand with a blue pencil. Still, it was not a bad paper and I enjoyed researching it in the National Library.

In the December 1948 number of the *National Student*, I had a piece of verse that said something of what I believed about college life:

Capability

Learn by rote the names of all the lads
The smile, the grip of hand on greasy hand.
These the tenuous rungs on which to climb -
To what? To fame, to human Christlike worth?

To get away - but how? - aye there's the rub
The hub of all the universe is here
The mecca of the madmen of the land
The intepseudollectual and the pub.
On the sixth he made a man and on the sixth -
That's Saturday - why, then we too make men -
Of mice - to vote or not to vote - aye there's the rub
The hub of all the universe is here.
To work, to mate, possess compatibility
To quicken life where there was none before.
Such thought, such action furthest from our mind.
The universal hub is capability
And we, but centripetal spokes - committee members.

That issue of the *National Student* (No. 104) shows me at my busiest. Not at the books, but I was auditor of the English Litt., hon. correspondence sec. of the L & H; on the committee of the Law Society when my friend Paddy Connolly, later Attorney General, was auditor; author of a recruiting article on the Pearse Battalion, F.C.A., which I had joined in March 1947, and a member of the S.R.C.

Jim was pretty mad at me for joining the "Free State Army" as Republicans called it. Yet when I set off for my first camp in Gormanstown, Co. Meath, he felt impelled to take a photograph of me in front of the house. I suppose I was a

Cartoonist unknown. The Literary and Historical Society in session. I'm the one with the letters. From the National Student, February 1949.

*At the inaugural of the English Literature Society in 1949. The speakers to my paper were
Senator Michael Hayes, John Dowling and Senator J.T. O'Farrell - Irish Times.*

classic approval seeker. Certainly I did not find it, but would learn from his
friends or an aunt how proud he was of some achievement of mine. I spent
twelve years in A company of the Pearse Battalion and was commissioned in
1952. It was an exciting life until alcohol took over completely and I would have
to tell my sergeant, Frank Bradley, to carry on while I went back to the billets for
a morning cure.

Being a Sunday soldier involved service on Tuesday nights, training on
Sunday mornings and attending annual camp in Gormanstown and later in
Kilkenny Barracks. Paidín O'Halpin, engineer, poet and randy drinker of some
distinction, was a company sergeant, and like R.N. (Bob) Hayes, a good soldier
by my definition. They had the gift of leadership and always seemed to be in
command of themselves. Paidín's father had died leaving a large family in Donegal
and Paidín bent his considerable talents to educating his siblings. Bob Hayes's
father Liam had been Adjutant - General in the Free State Army. Directness,
clarity and confidence were in the genes. I, though I was a "gildy" soldier and
ambitious enough, was not made in the same mould.

Where I excelled was in driving. In 1947, the FCA was supplied with the

"Woodie", the beautiful American-made Ford V-8 station wagon that was panelled in a pale timber that might have been ash. I was already driving my father's car, and when it came to doing the Army driving test, I had only one skill to master - the new steering-column gearshift. I spent some hours getting the hang of it in Seán Myler's garage in Fitzwilliam Lane and when the day came had to drive through Dublin with three Regular Army officers on the bench seat behind me. They stopped me on Knockmaroon Hill and told me to start from cold. There was no synchromesh on first gear, but I double declutched and she floated up the steep hill. I can still hear one of the officers saying to the others: "I think we have something here". They placed me first.

I was a menace on the road. After the 150th celebration of the 1798 Rising, we were driving home from a pageant in Cavan when we were stopped at Virginia by our training officer, Captain Benny Allen. "You", he said to BQMS Peter O'Neill beside me, "are drunk. And your driver is nearly as bad". That was the end of it, probably because Captain Allen was as intoxicated as the two of us put together. At any rate we heard no more.

One of our regular runs was to Clongowes Wood College, where a schoolboy unit of the Pearse trained on Sundays. We carried the Lee-Enfield rifles down from Portobello (Cathal Brugha) Barracks and tried to instil the elements of infantry training into lads whose main preoccupation was how to get into the long grass to have a smoke. One of these lads was Patrick Cooney, later to become a Fine Gael Minister for Justice, later still a right-wing member of the European Parliament.

I rose slowly through the ranks, doing an officers' training course in 1951-2. The day we were commissioned at Portobello, my parents were there. Less welcome to them than the "Free State" brass was the presence of Captain Séamus Kavanagh, who had been Officer Commanding H Company, First Battalion of the Dublin Brigade in September, 1920, when my uncle Kevin Barry was arrested. There was a story in the family that Kavanagh had failed to give the signal to withdraw from the ambush that eventually led to Kevin's being hanged in Mountjoy Jail. So the Barrys did not speak to Kavanagh, yet it was he who was photographed with me in the *Irish Press* next day. The family's version of the Church Street ambush was not true, as I try to show in my book on Barry [25].

After I became an officer, my drinking became worse. I would don a non-commissioned officer's greatcoat to have a pint with Peter O'Neill in the sergeants' mess. I would drink with the same Benny Allen our Training Officer in Bettystown or Laytown until three in the morning, always in uniform. This disgrace of the uniform led to my being carpeted by the Camp Commandant and warned. Still I would go to Dublin on my 125c.c. James motor-cycle and spend the day and night in Davy Byrne's pub, often in uniform. I thought I looked well in uniform, that the bars on my epaulettes gave me a special cachet. In reality, I was making a mockery of the superfine cloth that I was privileged to wear. (I gave my last uniform to the National Museum along with Kevin Barry's walking stick and a Sacred Heart scapular of his that my grandmother had pinned to my jacket to protect me).

Paidín O'Halpin, who married my cousin Mary Moloney, wrote one poem that I have always felt deserving of a wider public. It appeared in the *National Student* in April 1947, when Paidín happened to be chairman of the board of management. It was worth the page he gave it:

hick-hawk

For song, let the soldier sing:
The stars are fallen, the filigree unbound;
Torch lies unlit impressing the dust,
All oil long gone, uncommon loveliness changed.
These are they, living or dead, who knew
Bolt lift and latch, red flame speaking
In ditches dully, rapidly from rooftops.
We were then still unborn, coming after the green-clad,
The double-gunned heroes who gave us thought: after battle,
How we the unborn, the young hawks, small troopers,
Were the relief guard for her, the sun in our faces,
Well tricked with equipment Short Magazine Lee-Enfields:
We take over, gun slap, heel clack, sword shine.
And now Setanta is sullen: we cannot believe our fathers
Were once not ignorant, not always mouthers;
Were not as now we see them, elder men untrusting,
Brokers, pension claimers: we cannot believe
They saw without wonder the left side of his face.

So old men in the guard room, when our time
Shall come to die, no braver than you were,
Congregate and sing, all bulbed with tears,

Of raddled Éire; and when we shall die,
To let your bigots live, to guard your flag,
Shine out your bald heads bared for the old face:
But stay there in the guard room, that we can forget
The stars are down: let our whole thoughts be
Of where the steel sprang and the wind turned and
the competent helix was moving.

I liked that poem then: I like it now. The symbolism of seeing "without wonder" the flaw in Patrick Pearse's appearance - he had a cast in one eye - has not diminished in the fifty years since Paidín spoke.

CHAPTER 8

MY UNCLE DAN

We were an élite: I am conscious of that. We were not wasters. We all went on to make a contribution that was shaped by what we were and what we absorbed in those golden years. My father, as I have said earlier, sold Florenceville in 1947, leaving my mother shattered. He was tempted by the state of the housing market after the war and took the £5,500 that was offered by the Hills of Lucan, a textile family. We called it the Year of the Big Wind when Jim threw money around like snuff at a wake. He gave watches to my brother and myself and I got a pinstripe suit, my first and only, from F.X. Kelly in Grafton Street. We moved into a duplex apartment at No. 43 Fitzwilliam Square, and I moved into top gear in college society. No more ten shillings a week pocket money - out of which six shillings went on a weekly ticket to Harcourt Street Station by Drumm Battery Train. No more hurried kisses at the foot of the station steps as I ran to catch the last train home to Shankill at ten past eleven.

My brother moved to Glenstal, the most prestigious Catholic (Benedictine) school in the country; and my sisters walked down the road to the Sacred Heart Convent in Leeson Street. All this came to an end as it had to. The money burnt a hole in Jim's pocket. But it is not easy to forget having a key to Fitzwilliam Square and playing tennis there, or my 21st birthday party, a black-tie affair reported in *Social and Personal*. Seventy people came and Jim was the barman. Donal Barrington gave me a book on the Pre-Raphaelites which I treasure still, and a group of college friends clubbed together to get me a superb briefcase with DKO'D (K for Kevin) stamped on it. My uncle Dan borrowed this case (he was DJO'D) for a conference in Rome, where Seán Lemass, later Taoiseach, admired it. I pawned it a couple of years later but I was so fond of it that I redeemed it and it served me until it collapsed.

Bitterly though we bitched about UCD as a glorified technical school, we grew to love it and a few years afterwards deeply resented Michael Tierney's secret purchase of the big landed houses along the Stillorgan Road that came to be known as the Belfield Campus. There was enough land around Earlsfort Terrace to build on and to preserve the southern nexus of what de Valera called Dublin's cultural complex, running from Earlsfort Terrace through St. Stephen's Green down Kildare Street with its National Museum and Library and the National Gallery on Merrion Square down to Trinity College. Tierney's dream was to

The not-so-gildy soldier setting out for his first summer camp at Gormanstown, 1947.

isolate the college of Newman and the Jesuits and to ensure that his university became Dublin's primary seat of learning. It was a mistake, as many of the students (and staff) of that vast and sterile space in suburbia will testify. "Undesirable and unnecessary" was Donal Barrington's summary of the use of Belfield. He was President of Tuairim, an opinion forming group of UCD graduates formed about 1953 and by 1960 consisting of eight branches. Donal Barrington, now a judge of the Supreme Court, was one of the founder members, as I was. Dr. Patrick Moore, Professor Frank Winder and Brian Lenihan were the other names I recall. I especially remember objecting strongly to the name Tuairim (Irish for opinion) as being unsuitable for a group that aspired to inform a wide spectrum of people about the issues of the day. I was going through a very anti-Gaelic phase.

For me, the college had immediate connections. "The Faculty of Science", wrote John Dowling[26], "gave the IRA a member of the G.H.Q. staff in the person of James O'Donovan, the Director of Chemicals, who devised and organised the manufacture of the two explosives known playfully as 'Warflour' and 'Paxo' ". And: "On the 1st of November [1920], a young medical student named Kevin Barry, from the 1st Battalion, was hanged in Mountjoy. Then the storm burst . . . ." Kevin is remembered by a fine stained glass window by Richard King. It stands still in the old U.C.D. Council Room above the National Concert Hall.

Connections, connections. My grandfather was an excise officer, moving from Wakefield, where my father was conceived, to Roscommon, where he was born. Grandfather's next move was to Glasgow, where my father was educated by the Jesuits of St. Aloysius College. The family came to Dublin in 1914 and my father heartily disapproved of the Easter Rising, as did most of the country. It was Tom Dillon, his lecturer in chemistry at UCD, who recruited him into the Movement two years later. Dillon married Geraldine Plunkett, sister of Joseph Mary Plunkett, one of the poet leaders of the Rising. Geraldine in turn was the daughter of George Noble Count Plunkett, the antiquarian and Sinn Féin politician. The Rising after which his son was executed ended Count Plunkett's career as Director of the National Museum and led to his appointment as underground Minister of Foreign Affairs in 1919. His grandson, Michael Dillon the agricultural journalist, was a very dear friend to me, as is his widow Norah.

In the end of all, the degree of Bachelor of Arts of the National University of Ireland was conferred on me, my cousin Deirdre, my Barry cousin Paddy Moloney and my second cousin Jim Brennan in the autumn of 1949. I had done an honours course in Legal and Political Science, but I achieved only a pass.

To celebrate Dan O'Donovan brought us all down to Davy Byrne's moral pub for champagne. Dan my uncle had become very special for me. He stood for everything that was fun and smart and sophisticated. The youngest of my father's family, he was also the most handsome and successful. His Edwardian apartment on Earlsfort Terrace was purpose-built, had a lift and was most hospitable. He was generous in lending me his car - at that time a new Hillman Minx - and his wife Dorothy was a very kind hostess. When we lived in Shankill, I would go there before a dance ("dress dances" we called them) at the Gresham or Clery's or the Metropole, have a meal and be put to bed in the spare room to rest for a few hours. I could never sleep, but I was surrounded by what I regarded as really daring *Esquire* magazines so I spent the time profitably.

Dan's daughter Deirdre was adopted. He and Dorothy made the awful mistake of not telling her until she was twenty-one. The effect was predictable and may have hastened the alcohol problem that eventually killed her in 1982.

Dan, like Jim, had worked for Michael Collins in the War of Independence, and de Valera in the Civil

Daniel J. O'Donovan c. 1950

61

War, though Dan was not as prominent in either. Dorothy was one of the Brownes of Sligo, substantial Protestant merchants, so Dan got more work than Jim in the middle to late 1920s. Dorothy's older brother Frazer was elected to the Dáil in 1932 and served until 1937. Dan himself came into his own when Fianna Fáil took office in 1932. He became in turn private Secretary to Seán T. O'Kelly, Minister for Local Government and Public Health and a friend all his life; chairman of the National Health Insurance Society, where he was succeeded by Dr. Dignan, Bishop of Clonfert; County Commissioner for Dublin from 1941-1946; then first Secretary of the new Department of Social Welfare in 1947. He was, for a civil servant, a highly political animal, independent of mind and effective in action. When some zealous Catholics on his staff suggested to him that the working day should end with a decade of the Rosary he blew them out of the water, reminding them that the work of the State had nothing to do with devotional practices. I should add that some details of Dan's career are not easy to verify. Thom's Directory for 1955 is at variance with my recollections and other sources at some points, but they are not material.

As Dublin County Commissioner, Dan left his mark. Hickey and Doherty, those splendid historians, make no mention of him or the abolition of Dublin County Council in their "Dictionary of Irish History", [27] but his autocratic sign is inscribed on parts of the county's infrastructure.

The Irish Times [28] in 1943 noted a boat trip on the Upper Liffey. The occupants were Maurice Walsh, the novelist, T.S.C. Dagg, a former president of the Dublin University Boat Club, and the bould commissioner. The trip, he told his officials later, had shown him that the people of Dublin had at their door a great unspoiled pleasure way of whose beauty and amenities they were almost all ignorant. The newspapers traditionally used indirect speech, but I intend to shorten and sharpen the reporter's words:

It was a great revelation to me, and I hope to be able,
in consultation with those owning interests
on the river, to overcome the natural obstacles
in the way of pleasure boating. The cost would be
very small and the return in the form of
improved recreation facilities, especially for
the youth of the country, would be very great.

He looked to private enterprise to provide punts or boats, and if the public were interested he would proceed almost immediately with the next step.

That was as far as Dan could go. I don't think the project went much farther, but in the following year he told the members of the Tomorrow Club of a far-reaching plan [29] which is still being developed today - the transformation of all main traffic arteries radiating from Dublin into super-highways designed to carry traffic at a speed of 75 miles an hour.

"A vast £5,000,000 road improvement project" was envisaged. A large amount of the work "has already been accurately surveyed and detailed plans prepared".

That was in February 1944, past the turning point of the greatest war mankind has seen, yet in a couple of years the dual carriageways at White's Cross and The Big Tree at Loughlinstown were carrying traffic. He could hardly have foreseen the West Link or the planned tunnel from Whitehall to the docks, but he made an imaginative beginning to the solution of Dublin's traffic problems.

The first time he came to the notice of the public was when he succeeded in "requisitioning" the administrative floors of Busárus, the splendid new bus station designed by Michael Scott as headquarters for Córas Iompair Éireann (CIÉ, the State transport company).

The bus station survives as such to this day, but the tall office block attached to it became Áras Mhic Dhiarmada, the office of the Department of Social Welfare.

Dan's second essay in independence was not so successful. When Fianna Fáil was booted out of office in 1948 to be replaced by the first Inter-Party Government, the portfolio of Social Welfare was taken by the Tánaiste, William Norton, leader of the Labour Party. Norton appointed a civil servant, Seán O'Driscoll, as information officer. When it became apparent that Seán was mixing Labour Party work with his departmental duties, Dan suspended him. Norton instructed Dan to reinstate O'Driscoll. Dan refused on the grounds that he was acting in his capacity as accounting officer and not as Secretary of the Department. Norton prevailed on the Government (in the person of John A. Costello, the Taoiseach) to dismiss Dan. He was sacked amid a flurry of newspaper statements in which the warm personal relations between Minister and Secretary turned rancid. Dorothy and Uncle Joe Brennan, then Governor of the Central Bank, put out long press statements, the one to show how much at home Norton had been at No. 2 Earlsfort Mansions; the other to argue the legality of what had been done. Joe Brennan was a man of such caution, conservatism and rectitude that it took real courage for him to enter the lists in such a tournament.

Dan was out of a job until Fianna Fáil returned in June 1951, by which time a new Secretary had been appointed. A new position, Adviser to the Minister for Social Welfare, was created for Dan and soon when a vacancy arose he was made Secretary to the President - his old friend Seán T. O'Kelly. The reign of the twelve-year old Jameson was restored. Illness caused Dan to retire not long after Éamon de Valera replaced Seán T. in 1959, and he died in 1967 after years of suffering with the aftermath of surgery on his stomach, his halo in my eyes untarnished.

I had for a few years suspected that Dan was dallying. In the 1960s I got to know Ursula Wassermann, a Swiss journalist working in Geneva. She made several visits to Dublin and it was not until 1980, when I was attending a conference in Vevey, that I looked her up and made her tell me the whole story. It was worth the journey to Begnins.

In 1936, Dan took a Mediterranean cruise alone. On board was an attractive minor, Ursula Wassermann, travelling with her father. A friendship developed and it blossomed into love. On Ursula's 21st birthday, Dan took her to bed and most tenderly deflowered her. He was 36.

It did not end there. Before the curtain came down over Europe in 1939, the two visited the Lake District of England; and after the War they met again. Then Dan on some pretext brought Ursula to Dublin and introduced her to Dorothy. That, as many men dedicated to monogamy could have told him, was a mistake. But before he died, she did see Dan in Dublin again and I was able to give her some economic journalism work. She later married Harris Russell, a gentle American poet, and I saw them twice before Harris died.

That Mediterranean cruise should have borne another result. Before he sailed, a group of Dan's friends commissioned him to buy in Italy a suitable gift for them to mark the second marriage of Seán T.O'Kelly. His first wife Mary Kate had died and he married her sister Phyllis Ryan. The well-known Ryan family included Dr. Jim, another member of the Government; Denis McCullough's wife Agnes, and General Richard Mulcahy's wife Min.

From Italy, Dan brought home a fine female bronze figure. It was Dr. Ned O'Brien, the priest who had just given me my First Holy Communion, that recognised the statue as one of Fertility. Dan was laughed to scorn for his ignorance: the Ryan sisters had borne Seán T. no children.

CHAPTER 9

KARIN AND SEÁN

A t UCD, "doing a line" was our phrase for having a regular girl friend. I did a serious line with a very lovely woman called Maureen Duffy and thus we inspired in the "Social and Very Personal" column of the *National Student* the following:

SILVER WEDDING

DUNDUFFY. At their residence in Meath Street [where Maureen was teaching], Sergeant and Mrs Dunduffy, FCA, celebrated the Silver Jubilee of their wedding. A crowded house included their progeny to the fourth generation and relations of Mrs Dunduffy's first line.

Medical journals please copy.

Maureen Duffy (Mrs. David Keane) at the Nine Arts Ball in the Gresham Hotel, 1949.

Maureen's name - she later married David Keane, the architect and barrister who in 1996 was President of the Royal Institute of the Architects of Ireland - was linked with that of other men in the college magazine, as was Karin O'Sullivan's. I first met Karin in 1946, our first year at U.C.D. For the next eight years we had a stormy and volatile relationship as single people. Then we married and continued to have a stormy and volatile relationship until she died of cancer. The one thing we did right was to bring our daughter Kristin into the world.

Karin's strange history undoubtedly attracted me. She was the daughter of Pronnséas Ó Súilleabháin of Adrigole, Co. Cork and of Ilse Koehling of Eisenach in Thuringia. Pronnséas (the odd spelling was his own) was Chief Inspector of Technical Schools, an active member of the Gaelic League and a founder of the Save the German Children Society and of the Irish-German Society. He had degrees in several disciplines, was a doctor of philology of Freiburg and was called to the bar in 1949 with among others my UCD contemporary Anthony Cronin, the poet, writer and in the 1980s cultural adviser to Charles Haughey as Taoiseach.

Dr. Hermann Katzenberger, German Ambassador, with Pronnséas Ó Súilleabháin wearing the Verdienstkreuz of the Federal German Republic, about 1954.

Ilse O'Sullivan was also a philology doctor of Freiburg. She wrote her thesis on Shelley and the pair met at the university, marrying in 1926. The war of 1939-45 parted them. Karin and her brother Donal were attending Hermann Lietz schools in Germany and Ilse suffered from tuberculosis. So she went to her parents in Eisenach and spent several long periods in sanatoriums in Switzerland. Pronnséas spent the war without them in Dublin. He was a sociable, cheerful man of strong character, used to having his own way but lost in the delicate web of family relationships. When Karin and I got engaged, Ilse told him to discover if my intentions were honourable and my prospects rosy. We had a most uncomfortable meeting in the drawing room of 16 Oaklands Drive, Rathgar (now 31). We talked of anything but the matter at hand and I suppose Pronnséas told Ilse what she wanted to hear.

Our wedding day in 1954 was a social success and a personal calamity. The parish priest of Rathgar had first refused to marry us at all because Karin as a convinced atheist would have no truck with the Roman Catholic requirement to raise any children we might have as Catholics. He then said yes, but not in my church. You can have Beechwood Avenue or St. Joseph's, Terenure. We chose Terenure, which was the nearer to Karin's house, and we met Father Michael Frewen. He made further conditions. You can be married quietly in a side chapel with no music and there will be no question of a Papal Blessing. (Pius XII was Pope, and at that time a Papal Blessing was *de rigueur*). We talked to the organist and suggested that since the German Minister, Dr. Hermann Katzenberger, would be a guest it would be appropriate to play "Deutschland Ueber Alles" - the third verse of which as "Einigkeit und Recht und Freiheit", had recently been made the politically correct national anthem of the Federal Republic. The organist thought our idea sacrilegious until she conveniently discovered that there was a *Tantum Ergo* which shared the same melody.

It went like that, obstacles raised to be demolished, and we even got the time fixed for November 1st, All Saints Day, at 11o'clock. Thus a full church was assured, and at the end Father Frewen whispered: "I have decided to give you a Papal Blessing after all".

On the morning nothing would do me and my brother Gerry but to have a sizeable cure of brandy before the Mass. Afterwards, we had 120 guests at the Shelbourne Hotel, and I even made a passable speech thanking my parents quite sincerely for what they had done for me and the O'Sullivans for accepting me into their family. Gerry was my best man. Deirdre my cousin was Karin's bridesmaid and her best friend. And Karin had persuaded The O 'Rahilly and his wife, my aunt Elgin, to lend us their seven year old daughter Celie as her unwilling trainbearer.

The honeymoon was to begin in Amsterdam. Aer Lingus then flew to Paris and Amsterdam in mainland Europe only, so anyone trying to reach Germany had little choice. At any rate, the plane was delayed for hours, then cancelled. The party which had come to see us off got drunker and drunker. I remember my aunt Dorothy paying me a compliment of some kind, a thing she would never do sober. We set off for

A children's party at the Koehling house in Eisenach, Thuringia, c. 1934. Giving the Heil Hitler salute are Karin (front left) and Donal (fourth from left).

Germany the next day having spent our first night in the Gresham Hotel.

The Koehling family were well to do, and came originally from Westphalia. Ilse's father became director of a large and profitable kali (potash) mine in Thuringia and in 1933 bought a substantial house in Eisenach. The camera featured largely in their home life and recorded inter alia children's parties with the young ones saluting Adolf Hitler. Karin's and Donal's idyllic life was little affected by the War, and when Eisenach was taken and occupied by the Americans it was assumed that peace would reign over the land.

Then came the Potsdam Agreement of August 1945, under which the

Russians secured more of Germany and Berlin was quartered and became an island surrounded by the Russian Zone. Eisenach came under Russian hegemony. The elder Koehlings were put out on the road and for two years lived in a single room in the middle of the town. Ilse and the two children hitched a lift on an American jeep, spent some time in DP (Displaced Persons') Camps and six weeks later reached Paris, where Seán Murphy was the Irish Minister. Pronnséas had sent money but for some reason, Murphy

Ilse O'Sullivan-Koehling (Mutti) with her son Donal Gottfried (Goetz) outside the house at Eisenach in August 1934. The Adler Trumpf cabriolet steals the show. It pioneered front-wheel drive and had independent wheel suspension. Production began in 1932 and an Adler Trumpf, owned by Robert Briscoe and driven by R.B.S. Le Fanu, won the Bray "Round the Houses" motor race in 1934. Briscoe, later the first Jewish Lord Mayor of Dublin, was a staunch supporter of Fianna Fáil and a member of the Dáil. He was in the Four Courts garrison with my father when the Civil War began.

would not release the money and, having lived for a week on ice-creams, the O'Sullivans arrived in London to be met at the station by a warmly welcoming John Dulanty, the Irish High Commissioner to the United Kingdom. They settled down in Garville Avenue, Rathgar, until Pronnséas bought two new houses at the St. Luke's Hospital end of Oaklands Drive.

Because I could drive, I was asked to pilot one of Pronnséas's Mercedes 180s (he always bought things in twos - Austins A40s, Mercedes, houses, in the hope of making money, which he rarely did). We were to drive down to Shannon to pick up the old Koehlings. They had left Eisenach and decided to settle in Ireland. The GDR was not yet established and the Berlin Wall was fourteen years in the future, so a fluid, chaotic Central Europe offered them the opportunity to flee. All their possessions stayed in Eisenach where Donal, now living in Brisbane, Australia, has instigated proceedings to recover the house.

It was a surreal drive to the new airport at Rineanna. Tyres were scarce, so we had a few punctures to repair. Karin and Donal kept a strict eye on the speedometer which was not to move beyond 40 m.p.h. And on the way back there were two total strangers to me trying to assess what was alien territory to them.

Günter Schutz, one of the better-known German agents parachuted into neutral Ireland, photographed in the Gresham in February 1947 with Mona Brase, Erica Stieber, John Stieber, Karin and myself.

Within eleven years, the Koehling family was destroyed. The old man died of cancer in 1949; Pronnséas got a heart attack in 1956, a year after his retirement and two months too soon to greet his granddaughter Kristin. Ilse (Mutti) got a brain tumour in 1958 and within three weeks her mother died in Germany, again of cancer.

Karin herself lived only nine years more. Her married life was marred, you might say nullified, by my drinking, but she made a remarkable career for herself. She was gifted in many ways. She had spent a year at finishing school in Lausanne in 1950, and also after college trained at the Grafton Academy of Dress Designing. She made most of her own clothes and was well known for her good taste. Using her fluent German (virtually her mother tongue), she built up an interpreting and translation business. I can recall her description of the difficulties that Stephen O'Flaherty of Motor Distributors encountered when a team came from Wolfsburg to assess the quality of the paintwork on Dublin made Volkswagens. It was the first time I heard the technical term "orange peel".

Before we married, Karin spent about three years in the personnel department of Aer Lingus, where her manager was Michael Dargan, later to lead the airline. Her colleagues gave us a boxed set of Newbridge cutlery.

But *si monumentum requiris*, look at Amnesty International. Peter

Benenson, an English lawyer, wrote his now famous article, "The Forgotten Prisoners" in *The Observer* in 1961. Out of the reaction to that crusading piece, he founded Amnesty, of which Seán MacBride was one of the original trustees.

Seán MacBride and Karin met during the Fluoridation case, a *cause célèbre* which involved MacBride as senior counsel calling expert witnesses from abroad to give evidence showing the dangers of adding fluoride to the public water supply. Karin was the

Seán MacBride at a conference in Copenhagen about 1964

interpreter where the expert was German-speaking. They lost the case against the state and went on to fight the Singer case, which involved Dr. Paul Singer, a Czech philatelist who had launched Shanahan's Stamp Auctions in 1953 in Dublin. The business collapsed in 1959 with assets of £400,000 or so, and claims by investors and creditors of £2 million. The complex three year legal battle led to Dr. Singer's acquittal on charges of fraud. Richie Ryan, later Minister for Finance in the 1973-77 Coalition, was MacBride's able and hard-working solicitor, and I remember being very impressed by the extent to which he dipped into his own pocket to buy textbooks on fluoride.

To me MacBride was an enigma. A brilliant lawyer and, with or without his French accent, a charming man, he had the most romantic history of anybody at the Bar[30]. He was in and out of Oaklands Drive very often in those years and

it was plain that his relationship with Karin was quite close. By then I was living a more or less separate life. We shared a bed, but it was often empty on her side when she was abroad, and I was having affairs of my own. It was that tacit understanding which allowed me to enjoy Seán's company. In 1964 I got a free ticket to Zürich from Aer

Donal Barrington addressing an early meeting of Tuairim. Left is Paddy Kilroy.

Lingus and spent a week with Seán in Geneva. He was then Secretary-General of the International Commission of Jurists and staying at the Metropole overlooking the lake. He put me up there, and we had much good talk and food and of course drink. In a small family restaurant at Carouge, just out of Geneva, he introduced me to the delights of Raclette, a dish of new potatoes and cheese that I could not find again until I was in Lucerne years later. Seán, like Jack Lynch, was a man of great girth topped by a deceptively small head.

We spent the bones of a week in the West of Ireland too, when Seán was working on the Western Circuit. Through MacBride, I met John Willy O'Connor and Peter O'Malley, both to become circuit court judges. Peter was married to Mary Pat Cullen whom I had known at college. When it was time to come home, we filled the boot of Seán's car with oysters from Burke's of Clarenbridge and thus ensured a warm welcome at Oaklands Drive.

Years later, when I was working in the Bank of Ireland, I had an intriguing encounter with MacBride. Seán had suffered a heart attack long before Karin died. He was driving through Ballinasloe when it happened, and he was taken into the Portiuncula Hospital. The good nuns fell in love with Seán and he became their patron and protector whenever the Medical Council, the Department of Health or anybody else threatened their serenity.

In 1979, the hospital celebrated the opening of a new wing or nurses' home - I forget - by holding a large and lavish lunch. The Bank was advancing the money for the building, so I used their presence to invite myself. I think Seán had told me about it. Anyway I noticed that right through lunch he and Gaetano Alibrandi the Papal Nuncio were deep in converstaion.

When Bishop Tom Ryan of Clonfert and the other speakers had finished, we stood up to go. I went straight to Seán and asked what they had been talking about.

Karin in Amnesty mode, about 1965.

It was about the cardinal's red hat. Tomás Ó Fiaich, the Archbishop of Armagh and Primate of All Ireland, was reported to be about to be made a cardinal.

"The British", said MacBride, "have launched a strong campaign in the Vatican. They don't want him to get the hat because they regard him as a fellow-traveller of the IRA. The Nuncio is pushing very hard for Ó Fiaich and he wants me to help". It was a fairly dirty business culminating in yet another victory for Alibrandi. Louis McRedmond's dictionary[31], alluding to this aspect of Ó Fiaich's career and not to this incident says: "In fact Cardinal Ó Fiaich repeatedly denounced violence but this was noticed less than his protests against the mistreatment of prisoners . . ".

Seán and Karin founded the Irish Section of Amnesty in 1963, he as chairman and she as secretary. They travelled Europe to meetings and conferences. In 1966, she was asked to go to Berlin to write a risk-laden report on the conditions of prisoners of conscience in East Germany, and even when she was stricken with Hodgkins Disease in January 1967 she sustained great hopes of attending an executive meeting at Elsinore in March. Terry Keane the journalist helped her to choose a trouser suit that would conceal her skeletal legs and Charlie and Maureen Haughey graciously acceded to her request to visit her dressed for a formal entertainment. She still loved clothes but Elsinore had to do without her.

She was in the private nursing home of St. Vincent's Hospital in Leeson Street. I was given two months off work to be with her while she was dying. I spent most of that time philandering and drinking across the road in Kirwan's pub.

Seán MacBride was even less attentive. I never knew why. Her most devoted visitor was K.M., Mr. Justice T.C. Kingsmill Moore, a pillar of Amnesty and of rectitude. K.M. brought a snipe of champagne every day, even though Karin was able only for Complan, which she took because she wanted very badly to live. "I can't afford to be ill when there is so much to do", she told K.M.

She remained an atheist and I had the task of preventing the hospital chaplain from pestering her. His persistence was so insensitive that eventually I had to use unspiritual language to make my point. He and the sisters may have lost that battle, but when she died early on the morning of April 8 1967, they won the war. We (Terry Keane and her husband Ronan) knew the bell was tolling for Karin and when the telephone call came we went to the nursing home to find her tiny corpse beautifully laid out with the rosary beads twined around her crossed hands.

From the time of Kristin's birth, we had a German au pair girl. The first and most memorable was Trudi Ratsch, now Richardson and still a mischievous friend. I can also recall Lotte Brase, a cousin of Mona Brase, the only daughter of Colonel Fritz Brase, the founder of the Army School of Music and an early member (1932) of the Nazi Party. Mona was Karin's first friend in Ireland. Lotte came back from Germany when Karin was dying and she was the reason I was able to pay so little attention to Kristin during that troubled time. But I had to think of some arrangement for her eleventh birthday on April 6. It was Lilo (Mrs L.M.) Stephens who hit on the idea of telling Kristin nothing about Karin's death until she and kindly Sybil Le Brocquy had held a children's party for her in the Dublin Zoo. That was on the afternoon

Karin's bust by Professor Friedrich Herkner of the College of Art, 1954. Herkner was appointed to the chair of sculpture in 1938, served in the German Army, and rejoined the college in 1947. A Sudeten German, he was a member of the Nazi Party, whose leader in Dublin was Adolf Mahr, the Director of the National Museum of Ireland.

of April 8 and when the last child went home I told Kristin that her mother was gone. She did not seem to take it in and indeed she was thirty years old before she did her real grieving.

I was surrounded by kindness (except for Jim, who refused to lend me his car for the funeral. When I think now of the alcoholic haze in which I lived through those months, I cannot blame him). Paddy Connolly offered me his Volkswagen Beetle for the few days and I only bumped it once. Father Austin Flannery, O.P., received her remains to his church, St. Saviour's in Dominick Street, and I remember with deep gratitude the fatherly hug that he gave Kristin in the chapel.

"Members of the Oireachtas, the Judiciary, the Diplomatic Corps, the legal profession, the Dublin newspapers and Radio and Teilifís Éireann" was how *The Irish Times* described the attendance at the funeral to Glasnevin Cemetery. I barely remember.

An appreciation by "Saracen and A.K.M." appeared in *The Irish Times*. Saracen was the pen name of Mr. Justice Kingsmill Moore, and Alexander was his equally active and loving wife. They began:

A great company in many lands should now be mourning her; but few will hear of her death, and the voices of those who do will not be heard, for they lie behind bars, isolated from human communication because they had the strength to form their own convictions, the courage to express them . . .

In the eyes of the Kingsmill Moores, Karin was "a woman of exceptional ability, with a mind that worked with the speed and accuracy of a computer, great administrative power, and profound judgment in dealing with the complicated and delicate problems which the work of Amnesty requires". They spoke of her enthusiasm and personal charm, and of her influence in the inner circles of the organisation. And they reminded me as I recently read their words - if, indeed, I had ever known - that she had been planning wider activities, expanding the skill she had shown as a girl in crafting poetry and writing essays. K.M. and Alexander ended their appreciation with Webster's line:

Cover her face; mine eyes dazzle: she died young.

She was 38.

CHAPTER 10

THE SUNDAY INDO

When I graduated in 1949 the job scene was dire. The pressure to work towards getting a place in the Department of External Affairs eased off and realistically my family and I began to regard journalism as a desirable end. I knew I could write and I enjoyed placing words. The difficulty was to get into a newspaper.

I had no false pride and while I waited took what the Labour Exchange offered. I sold muttoncloth and other automotive products - a lot of Douglas Holt remedies for burst radiators and things - for elderly Mr. Robertson, well known in the motor trade. He had a car which I could use for sales to garages by day and could rent from him as a "passion wagon" - the phrase we used - by night. He charged me 11/2d. a mile and never let me off fifty yards. When I had exhausted my personal contacts such as Owen Hayes of LSE Motor Company on North Frederick Street and Seán Myler of Fitzwilliam Lane, I ceased to be of use to Mr. Robertson, who let me go. My pay packet of £2 a week went down to nought.

The Labour Exchange (in Werburgh Street) sent me to 91B Rathgar Road, where Colonel Osborne, an ex-British Army officer, managed Wilkins and Mitchell Ltd., the Servis washing machine operation in Ireland. He too paid £2, plus 2s. 6d. bonus per machine delivered. We covered the country in no particular pattern, usually his daughter Barbara or a nice woman from Annagassan, Co. Louth and myself. Sometimes just myself. We carried the machines with us and called in to the dealer first. Magees of Ardee, Fitzgerald's of Cork and Hilliards of Killarney are three names I remember well, but there must have been a dozen.

They would direct us to the housewife who had expressed an interest in having a demonstration, and it was up to me to sell the product, which was the first washing machine to heat the water itself.

It was a harsh winter in 1949-50. Our two vans were decrepit, a Ford Ten and an Austin Ten, neither possessing either a heater or a spare tyre. I learned a lot about punctures and the repairing of them, and I sometimes had to endure 5.30 a.m. starts and windscreens icing up on the inside. I learned a little about Monaghan women. They piled up three weeks' laundry when they knew someone was coming to wash it for them. I learned the roads of Ireland fairly well too.

I suppose I stuck that job for three months until Colonel Osborne got the idea that I was over-qualified. In other words, I was not going to make it as a salesman.

The next job (also at £2 a week) came through a personal contact. David Coughlan was a well-known Bray businessman and the owner of Mr. What, the English Grand National winner. His son Sam had been at Glenstal with my brother Gerry and I think that is how I became the supervisor in Mr. Coughlan's souvenir factory at the harbour in Bray. The gruff and cynical manager was Tony Inglis, well known in the theatre as a stage designer. He and I got on well, especially over a liquid lunch at the Harbour Bar. The staff was mainly girls of fifteen or sixteen. They knew very little about their boring job filling, setting and dismantling the resin filled plaster moulds of Blarney Castle which then had to be painted and decorated with a small chip of "real stone" from Blarney. Every Friday I read off my list of slackers who had to go and endured the pitiful cries of "Ah mister don't sack us. Me mammy 'll kill me".

We had snow in May in 1950. It fell through a hole in the roof of the factory. But it could snow all summer as far as I was concerned, for I had landed a job in newspapers. I was to be a cadet sub-editor on the *Sunday Independent* and to be paid five guineas a week. I suspect that E.A. (Ned) Lawler, the first public relations officer in Europe and a former political correspondent of the *Irish*

The motor-cyclist 1950

Independent, was influential in placing me. He had worked for the ESB from its beginning in 1927 and my father knew him well.

On Monday May 15, 1950, I presented myself to Mr. Hector Legge, legendary Editor of that Sunday paper. Hector was tough, smiling when he judged it appropriate, tall and terrifying. He sat alone in his office, the rest of us all in one room. Like a movie-star journalist, he wore a white eyeshade, green on the inside. John Honohan was the meek and mild chief sub-editor who taught me all there was to know about sub-editing. ("John, it says in the radio programmes 'Tis Pity She's a Whore'." "Just put: '8 o'clock, play".) Next in seniority to Mr. Legge (he was the kind of man to whom one said mister) was Noel Moran, assistant editor, who shocked me by calling the Bishop of his native Waterford "an ecclesiastical bollox" Then there was Paddy Gavin, who had a club foot, a bad temper and a heart of gold, and the two unrelated Murphys, Michael and Dick. Dick and I became friends, sharing the same anti-clerical feelings and the same taste for Guinness. Saturdays were our busy days, starting at 10 a.m. and ending at about 2 the next morning. In the break between editions, Dick would mount the pillion of my motor-bike and we would head for the Boot Inn near the airport. The Boot was a "bona fide", a pub where travellers could get a drink after the city pubs had closed. *Bona fide* travellers of course, who lived five miles away at least.

Hector Legge's brother Arthur was the sports editor, so different from Hector that we decided Hector had learned his grand accent from Pelmanism. The first time I sought permission to go to the lavatory, I heard from Dick Murphy afterwards, Arthur turned to the room and said in his querulous flat Kildare accent: "I wonder what that fella failed at?" It was a measure of the respect which journalism enjoyed that he thought I, with my pin-stripe suit and incipient blond moustache, must have been drummed out of something better.

It was a good summer. The printers went on strike and to keep me busy, John Honohan sent me to see what stories I could dig out from attending the UCD summer school. She was a pleasant Finnish girl, I did write about her, and it was good to be back in academe.

The strike over, I was put to serious sub-editing, headlines, layout, subbing down stories for our sister paper, the *Irish Weekly Independent*, which was specifically a subscription paper for exiles, especially in America. I felt I was on my way.

But pints cost money and five guineas (I honestly do not remember whether

I gave my mother some of my salary, which means I probably did not) did not buy enough. So I got night work checking crosswords. The *Sunday Independent* crossword was a national institution with a distinguished jury that included Dr. Michael Tierney of UCD, substantial cash prizes and the possibility of submitting multiple entries. For us it was slavery under Mr. Aylward the slave-driver. Productivity was the goal and exits to the lavatory were monitored. Even so, I could get downstairs to the Oval Bar, consume a pint, and be back in my place quickly enough not to be noticed. The only trouble was that a pint (or two) could make me sleepy, and mistakes were punished by reductions in pay, suspension or dismissal, depending on the size of the mistake. I did a couple of years of this drudgery and I can say that the only good thing that came out of it was friendship with Paddy Downey, the learned and lovely gentleman who became the lyrical G.A.A. correspondent of *The Irish Times.*

We were living then in Whitehall Lodge, Rathfarnham, a house beside the Bottle Tower near Hughes's Dairy. Hall's Barn, to give the Bottle Tower its proper name, was erected during "the hard frost" of 1741-42 to give work to the poor. It was, says Weston St. John Joyce[32], "obviously built in imitation of 'The Wonderful Barn' near Leixlip". These barns used as grain stores are conical and have spiralling outside staircases. I felt fortunate to live in sight of such a piece of famine history, built a century before the Great Hunger. I had in earlier years enjoyed the daily view of the Obelisk dominating Killiney Bay and dating from the same harsh winter. The cone or sugar loaf shape seems to have been fashionable. And of course I now live almost under the shadow of the Great Sugar Loaf mountain.

The curious thing, I find, is that people have forgotten what a sugar loaf is. I found and bought them when they were still being sold in the German Democratic Republic in the 1960s, cones of hardpacked sugar about eight inches high and quite difficult to chip. By happenstance I found an image of the sugar loaf in Brittany in 1996. In the splendid Musée des Beaux-Arts in Quimper is a painting of the French School of the 17th century entitled "Fraises dans un saladier". Beside the bowl of strawberries is a sugar loaf partly used and wrapped in paper.

Whitehall Lodge, which I left to get married, was a modern house of great charm. It had a brook running through the grounds and Haggie Knight at the end of it. Haggie lived in a little house with no telephone, so we

The strawberries and the sugar loaf at Quimper.

78

frequently heard her loud conversations on our telephone. The most memorable were with her theatrical friends and especially Mícheál MacLiammóir. She was an aunt of Patrick Campbell (later Lord Glenavy), the *Irish Times* columnist and comic writer, and of Michael Campbell, the author of "Lord Dismiss Us" [33], a novel about St. Columba's College and the gay goings on of that public school. In another of his books he has faithfully depicted his

Sheila at the Bottle Tower, Whitehall Lodge, 1952.

aunt, "Peter Perry,[34] a six-foot elderly Bohemian lady living on the gaudy fringes of Dublin theatrical life".

Jim rented Whitehall Lodge, which was not for sale. He had suffered a severe sciatic illness in 1949 and though he made a good recovery and went back to work, his experiences in the internment camp were taking their toll. Slowly he developed disseminated sclerosis and by the time he bought 114 Rathgar Road and his first new car, his mobility was considerably reduced. His dying began in the middle 1960s and he had to spend ten years in his last prison, the nursing home called Our Lady's Manor in Dalkey, before in 1979 he achieved the death he longed for.

CHAPTER 11

GOERTZ DEPARTS

My filial piety dwindled as I imprisoned myself in a bottle. I visited Monty and Jim as seldom as possible, especially as they did not like Karin. Nor did Karin willingly spend time with them. Sunday was Karin's day of rest, so Kristin and I would go to Mass in Rathmines, and beg lunch or some social contact from friends. My aunt Minnie in Dún Laoghaire was good for a glass of sherry. David and Maureen Keane sometimes gave us lunch in Baily.

I had no motor-car. The great driver was without wheels. My rationale was that taxis and buses were better suited to my urban life. The truth is that the money I would have spent on a car was better spent on a more worthy cause. Karin's mother - we lived in Oaklands Drive in her converted upper floor from 1956 - paid for a new NSU scooter which I exchanged a few years later for a Berkeley sports car. I wager that you never heard of a Berkeley. I bought it from Huet's Garage, where they told me it had been owned by the son of E.J. Moeran the composer. It had a fibre-glass body and a most unreliable 322 c.c. British Anzani engine. Quite smart and quite useless. Kristin used to vomit out of the child's seat/luggage compartment.

It was 1968 when my sainted sister Sheila told me I ought to have a car. She lent me £150 from her children's Post Office savings and I bought for £300 a second-hand Mini from Denis Tierney (one of the twins) of the L.S.E. Motor Company. It was a great source of pride and enabled me to take my father to the dentist, that decent man Joe Briscoe whose father Bob had been in the Four Courts garrison with Jim at the beginning of the Civil War; and to bring him to get his ears syringed by Mr. Wood in Sir Patrick Dun's Hospital. These were painful outings. Jim was availing himself of the only transport in the family. He was chairbound and the Mini was not ideal. And I was usually hung over, though now and then we achieved some rapport and I was glad to stop on the way back to Dalkey to get him a Baby Power. He drank a lot of whiskey in those years, but it was to kill pain. I do not believe that he was alcoholic.

My mother went to see him every day while she was able. As with her visits to the Curragh, she was confined to buses. When she too had to go to live in Our Lady's Manor, she would spend hours in his room, with him making it painfully obvious that he did not welcome her company. If she had stayed away from him, I think he would have had another ground for complaint. It was a god awful time for both of them and I deeply regret that I did not do more to entertain them or make it easier to die with dignity.

Their fiftieth wedding anniversary in 1976 was, however, quite an event. All the family who could come were there in the residents' room of the home and the nuns arranged good food and drink. Mac (The O'Rahilly) had by this time become treasurer of the senior O'Donovans' finances, a job that I should have undertaken. He had quite a task. The Manor was one of the most expensive homes in Dublin and I was not the most reliable contributor to Mac's funds. It was very onerous for him and if he and I did not always work in harmony, he did all the paperwork and conducted all the business with the bank. Posthumously I acknowledge a deep debt of gratitude to a man of quixotic ideals and generous interest.

Mac O'Rahilly, *is mór an trua*, wrote Jim's obituary for *The Irish Times*[35]. I say it's a pity because it does not show me the father I knew. But Mac was

dealing with the public man, "a man of honour and courage. He was unpopular, as he did not suffer fools gladly or at all".

Mac calls Jim a true follower of Patrick Henry Pearse. "Both men worshipped heroes: Pearse - Cuchullain and Wolfe Tone; O'Donovan - Casement and Pearse". But Mac treats too lightly of the Seán Russell era. What he says is that "O'Donovan was interned at the Curragh during the second World War. Some of those interned had little to do with anything". That is all: no S-Plan, no Abwehr, no Goertz. No

Captain C.D. (Kit) Wood, our training officer about 1952, when I took this photograph at Gormanstown Camp.

mention of Monty and his family either.

I am in danger of forgetting Goertz myself. He was finally caught in October 1942, brought to Arbour Hill and sent to join the other German agents in Athlone Barracks until 1946. When he was free, he came to see us at Florenceville a number of times. During one of his visits, he presented me with his gun, his parachute knife and fifty rounds of ammunition.

The gun, as I have said, was an FN Browning .32 automatic, a classic Belgian pistol designed 50 years before. To my unpractised eyes at least, it looks exactly like one of the guns in the 1916 section of the National Museum and attributed to Pearse. I expended most of the rounds alone on the summit of Carrigolligan or in the company of Captain C.D. (Kit) Wood when he was training officer of the Pearse Battalion. I had four or five rounds left when in 1975 the gun, ammunition and knife were burgled from our house at Cashel, Kilbride, Bray. I did not report the burglary to the guards because I had no licence for firearms. The gun's present whereabouts are known.

Kristin and the Berkeley at the gates of St. Lukes

Goertz I remember as a fine old gentleman, something of a hero to a seventeen-year-old. But he was a sick man and a bitter man, striving for self-vindication and appalled that his superior, the former chief of Abwehr II, Erwin von Lahousen, had appeared as a witness for the prosecution in the Nuremberg War Trials [36]. He could not decide whether to return to Germany or try to settle in Spanish Morocco. In February 1947 he became secretary of the Save the German Children Society, for which I was a flag-seller a couple of times.

The Save the German Children Society led to Operation Shamrock, the name given to the Irish Red Cross Society's arrangement to bring to Ireland 400 German children, some orphaned, some fatherless, some lost, all malnourished. They were housed first at St. Kevin's Hostel, Glencree, a gaunt barracks built about 1800 to open up the Wicklow Mountains to the Redcoats seeking Michael Dwyer and his men after the 1798 Rising.

Among the 400 was Ernst-Albert Dirksen, taken from Glencree and fostered by my uncle Peter O'Donovan (another Excise man) and his wife Ethel Bouchier-

Hayes. They had no children of their own and were happy to bring up Ernst as our cousin. He went to Belvedere, worked in Nigeria and England, and speaks not a word of German.

Ernst was among the survivors of Operation Shamrock brought together at Glencree in March 1997 for a jubilee. There was much hugging and remembrance and laughter and crying over the two days. The German President Roman Herzog and the Irish President Mary Robinson were the principal guests at a moving service at St. Patrick's, Cathederal. The German Embassy, the Red Cross, the Civil Defence, the Garda Síochána and the Department of Foreign Affairs made the homecoming memorable for all of us. I and my sister Sheila were proud that weekend to be Irish, and to welcome Ernst's English-Scottish wife Jan into the family. I showed the visitors Hermann Goertz's headstone in the German War Cemetery in that serene place.

Hermann Goertz's funeral at Dean's Grange Cemetery, photographed by The Irish Times on 27 May 1947. The swastika flag belonged to Goertz, whose obsequies were conducted by the Rev. K.D.B. Dobbs. My father can be seen in the doorway of the Protestant mortuary chapel. Anthony Deery, Goertz's IRA wireless operator; Werner Unland, and Charles McGuinness were also present. Dr. Eduard Hempel had been told by the Irish Government that his attendance would not be approved of.

Hermann Goertz and the other former internees were suddenly arrested in April 1947 and taken to Mountjoy Jail. It emerged that the Allies had demanded the extradition of the agents so that they could be questioned on German soil. De Valera agreed and a storm of accusations and justifications arose, Frederick Boland of External Affairs assuring Goertz that he had nothing to fear. Nevertheless, four of the Germans were flown from Baldonnel airfield to Frankfurt for interrogation. Goertz was paroled.

Whatever went on in Goertz's mind, on 23 May 1947, he made a routine visit to the Aliens Office at Dublin Castle to renew his parole. There he was told that he was to be

Hermann Goertz's headstone as it stood in Dean's Grange Cemetery - Irish Times

removed later that day to Mountjoy. He went on smoking his pipe and seemed quite calm until one of the two detectives in the room saw him put something in his mouth. When a detective took a small phial from Goertz's open mouth, he asked Goertz what he had taken. "None of your business", said Goertz, and a few seconds later collapsed. He died in Mercer's Hospital of potassium cyanide poisoning.

His funeral to Dean's Grange was large. His coffin was draped in a swastika and covered in a sea of flowers. Jim O'Donovan was there, as the press photographs attest. At an inquiry held in Frankfurt, John A. Costello, S.C., one year later to be Taoiseach, asked if he could speak. "I ask you", he pleaded, " to give for your verdict merely a finding as to his death and nothing that will besmirch his ideals or his honour".

The headstone, said to have been carved by himself, was erected over the grave. His remains and the remarkable stone were later removed to Glencree, Co. Wicklow, where he rests in peace today.

Dr. Hans Gilg, my good friend from Bruchsal, who has a long-standing interest in Ireland. When he retired about 15 years ago, he began to organise and lead special-interest tours to lesser-known areas of this country, and on a few occasions Jenny and I were able to entertain his groups to brown bread, smoked salmon and whiskey at Kilbride Lodge. He has a special interest in Operation Shamrock.

CHAPTER 12

MICKY ON THE MAINLAND

Michael Gill was an old pal from college. His family owned - still owns - Gills of 555 North Circular Road, where I had often met his father, mother, brothers and sisters, had often had a drink after hours, and had sometimes been lent Mr. Gill's big Wolseley for skites around the county with Michael.

Michael (Micky) came with me to attack the Continent of Europe in 1951. We began at Amsterdam, still the Aer Lingus gateway to Germany, where we expected to meet Karin O'Sullivan at Wiesbaden, where she was working at an up-market boutique. Our first surprise was that there was a distinct difference between London dry gin and genever, that you do not add orange juice to genever. You may, but the result is revolting. That experiment was conducted at the Pickwick Club on the Leidseplein in Amsterdam. If we knew of the red light district, we did not visit it. On the train east we were carefully inspected by the customs officers looking for coffee. Coffee was the currency, the scarcest commodity in post-war Europe. We managed to conceal the few pounds of coffee we had and got drunk on the dining-car wine.

At Frankfurt Station, I was astounded to see a little old woman in the men's lavatory, and outraged when she demanded a few pfennigs for two sheets of toilet paper. I had never heard of a *Wartefrau*, never mind paid one, in the one place I thought men were absolutely safe from women.

We had a romantic holiday in Wiesbaden despatching Micky to different attractions so that we could be alone. The difficulty was that Micky and freedom spelt trouble. He met up with American airmen and one night tried to auction his passport in a nightclub. He was rescued by a decent Romanian with a piece of shrapnel sticking out of the top of his head, and brought to a hostel. Micky was quite contrite when we found him but ready for more when we were not looking. The day we all went to Frankfurt, we missed the last train home, had to stay in the waiting room of the Hauptbahnhof and were able to observe the wretched bundles of humanity that stretched out on the floor clutching their cardboard cases while they awaited the next police raid. It was part of a refugee pageant being played out in railway stations all over Europe. Another discovery for me was to find at least one radio station that broadcast classical music all day. Germany was beginning to get a grip on me and I expanded my knowledge of the language.

I was motoring along nicely in my chosen profession. A couple of reporting jobs came my way, such as the baby Elizabeth Browne case, which involved my going to Corporation Street flats on a Saturday night to talk to her parents. I shall not forget the nasty smell of the Brownes' flat, or the grease-laden cap which had lived on his newsboy's head for about twenty years. Call it snobbery, but I had to learn somewhere that there are real live suffering people behind these municipal walls.

About 1951, I became the *Sunday Independent* second-string drama critic. This was to cover the basement theatres such as the Globe, the Mercury, the 37 Theatre Club that left Baggot Street to play over a shop in O'Connell Street. Through this exciting extra work I got to meet Barry Cassin, Nora Lever, Anna Manahan, Godfrey Quigley, Norman Rodway, T.P. McKenna, and above all Donal Donnelly, a part-time soldier like myself and a raconteur of epic proportions. I never lost my admiration for that man, whose part in the film "Korea" (1995) was a wonder to behold.

My interest in theatre came from my parents. I wouldn't call them inveterate first-nighters, but they saw everything worth seeing in the Gate and the Abbey ("Sodom and Begorrah" as the Dublin wits called them, the Gate being the home of Micheál MacLiammóir and Hilton Edwards, Dublin's much loved gays, and the Abbey being the National Theatre, devoted then to second-rate plays about cabins and peasants and turf-fires. I am generalising wildly: there were good Abbey shows such as Frank Carney's "The Righteous Are Bold", and there was Austin Clarke's Lyric Theatre on Sunday nights. I first saw Clarke's "The Second Kiss" there.) And the Gate had suffered the traditional Irish split. Edwards-MacLiammóir had fallen out with Lord Longford and his writer/playwright wife Christine, whose Longford Productions took over the Gate for six months in the year, mainly doing period plays. The nation was well served by these companies and there were others such as Alan and Carolyn Simpsons' Pike Theatre which gave us "Waiting for Godot", Beckett's masterpiece.

The uneven tenor of my courtship of Karin O'Sullivan went on to the accompaniment of corrosive jealousy on my part when she took an interest in Paddy Connolly, later to become Charlie Haughey's Attorney General and the genesis of GUBU, which entered the language as a result of Paddy's involvement with the murderer Malcolm Mac Arthur. Some years after Karin and I married, I was in the Buttery of the Royal Hibernian Hotel when for no reason that I could see or hear, Paddy punched my jaw. I fell flat on the floor and next day was presented by a messenger with a crate of good spirits and wines. There was a note from Paddy saying he was sorry the note was not in his own writing: he had broken his thumb on my jaw and had to get someone else to write the note. This was the same Paddy who graciously lent me his motor-car when my father refused to lend me his, for Karin's funeral.

In 1952, Karin had a fling with the Baron Oswald von Richthofen, counsellor of the German Legation and a nephew of the famous Luftwaffe air ace. I was so consumed with jealousy of this tall, elegant and well-to do diplomat that I followed them one night to the door of Jammet's Restaurant, then Dublin's smartest eating spot. Reckless with rage, I found a usable public telephone and had Karin paged. When she answered, I said I knew where she was and took a poor view of her conduct.

Little good it did me, until von Richthofen offered me a most lavish tour of Germany, the implication being that I would write nice things about a country trying desperately to rehabilitate itself in the eyes of a wary world watching how the new European Coal and Steel Community would fare in the search for permanent peace. I already was a committed European, having been indoctrinated by Professor John O'Mara of UCD, who had tried hard to get me into the ranks of the European Movement. To me, drink seemed preferable, but I accepted the German tour of three weeks.

Munich was a fairyland of art galleries and museums. In Regensburg, a press conference resulted in the truthful headline in the local paper telling the readers that "Mr. O'Donovan Likes to Drink Bavarian Beer". Valhalla with its busts of historical and mythical figures was visited in a magical motor-car, the open-topped Horch tourer belonging to the Prinz von Thurn und Taxis. I didn't meet him, so I assume he was doing his bit for tourism by lending his beflagged motor to the influential visitor from Ireland. It was a great tour which yielded the poor Germans nothing. I did not write a line. Such gratitude.

Thirty years after that epic journey, I wrote a poem about the leader of the Social Democrat Party, who died when I was in Bavaria. It was the time of *ohne Mich* (without me) a slogan which summed up the political stance of German Socialists. Have your atomic bomb and your NATO alliance and your American capitalism, it said, but without me. Count me out. The SPD changed from being left-wing and courageous to being centrist and putting power before principles. Here it is:

Germany 1952

When the bus driver switched on the radio
Kurt Schumacher died for me,
The early-morning news loudspeaking
The end of ohne Mich and ban the bomb
It was a time to hate America
Once again. Ban the bomb
And Bonn the Bundesdorf
And Yankee go home to hell

No NATO here we said
In the early morning of the day
Kurt Schumacher died -
And killed the dream he made

The one-armed dream he dreamed
In Dachau where they hurt him
And hurt his prisoned eyes
And left his vision unimpaired

So we learnt to unban the bomb
And unwrap the bundled dollar
And so far our wars have been little ones
With only ten million dead.

I was developing a great thirst for travel and the following year 1953, went to Paris, where I stayed with my cousins Deirdre O'Donovan and Katherine Moloney, who in 1967 married the poet Patrick Kavanagh. The third tenant of the apartment was Thérèse Campbell, who was to marry another poet, Anthony Cronin. Thérèse and Deirdre, both graduates, were hostesses with Aer Lingus. Our regular tipple at the Ile St. Louis was a bottle of wine costing one shilling at the grocer's across the road. You brought an empty bottle and he filled it from a barrel.

CHAPTER 13

DEV HUMBLED

N ever mind France. The greatest event of 1953 was the death of my grandmother. Nana was 82 when she died in the Bon Secours Hospital in Glasnevin. The house I had loved in Fleet Street was gone, rebuilt as part of an office block, and she had spent her last years in a cold-water attic flat in No. 3 Molesworth Street, now also demolished and reinvented as offices. She was a widow for 45 years and had brought up her seven children in central Dublin. Born across the road from Tombeagh, the Barry house she married into, she spent part of every year in Tombeagh, where her grandson Kevin farms the family holding between Hacketstown and Rathvilly to this day.

She was the mother of Kevin Barry, my mother's brother, who was hanged in Mountjoy Jail in November 1920. He was charged with the murder of a British soldier during an ambush at Monk's Bakery on Church Street. The story of his part in the ambush is told in my book, "Kevin Barry and His Time".

Nana's funeral was from St. Teresa's Church, Clarendon Street, to the place where she was born. It was huge. Principal among the congregation was Éamon de Valera, who stood against the outside wall of the church to greet the mourners. The Taoiseach was accompanied by his aide-de-camp, Colonel Seán Brennan. But, heads held high and full of contempt for their Prime Minister, the Barry clan marched past the man they would have died for in the Civil War. I was not proud to be a Barry that day. I still regard de Valera's presence there as a courageous act: he must have known the humiliation that he was risking.

Civic Guards saluted the cortège along the 50 mile route to Tinneclash, the family burial ground, and the people of Dublin, Wicklow and Carlow lined the roads. Jim Moloney had asked me to drive some members of the Moloney clan to Tombeagh in a car that he had hired. I got very drunk at the wake and drove back to Dublin in a disgraceful condition. In Abbey Street, the barman in the Oval Bar refused to serve me. It was the first and last time I was barred and I was most fortunate to have piloted the Moloney car safely home. It was a poor way to pay tribute to my grandmother, who used to tell me now and then that she was proud out of me. I don't think she had much Irish, but she used that Gaelicism and also pronounced her Dowling maiden name as Doolan (Ó Dúnlaing).

Politics fascinated me from the beginning. With Michael Gill I was an early member of Clann na Poblachta, the party founded in 1946 by Seán MacBride, Noel Hartnett, Jack McQuillan and Michael Kelly, who was general secretary. The treasurer was my uncle, The O'Rahilly. Fianna Fáil had been 14 years in office and had become tainted by patronage, corruption and scandal. A number of students, Republicans, small farmers and teachers formed the backbone of the new party which responded to a national need for social reform and economic expansion.

I worked for Mac Bride in the County Dublin by-election of 1947, canvassing and on election day driving a Ford Ten belonging to Seamus Laverty of *The Irish Times* to bring voters to the the polls. We were elated by MacBride's election. The party simultaneously won a by-election in Tipperary and de Valera began to run scared. He called a general election for 1948 and against all the odds the Clann won ten seats. In an extraordinary coalition of interests, five opposition parties combined to form the first Inter-Party Government.

MacBride became Minister for External Affairs and Dr. Noël Browne received the Health portfolio. I don't want to enter into the cauldron of bitterness engendered by the Mother and Child Scheme which wrecked the Government three years later, but I was appalled by the split caused in Clann na Poblachta and what looked like MacBride's treachery towards Browne. I have revised my view now and would suggest that students of the period should balance Noël Browne's autobiography "Against The Tide" [38] against James Deeny's memoirs of a chief medical officer [39].

I firmly decided not to let my political feelings intrude on my journalistic work, and thus, as I shall relate, belonged to no party from 1950 until 1971, when I changed professions for a spell. Impartial I was not: I disliked the aura of

Fine Gael because of where I came from, and Labour held no attraction for me. But the personal appeal of some politicians I successfully kept separate from their parties. Topmost among these special people was John Kelly, the oratorical genius whose independent spirit people of all opinions cherished. Like Karin, with whom he shared a special friendship and a love of Bach and Wodehouse and Myles na Gopaleen. John died young in 1991, a loss not only to his wife Delphine and his children but to the nation to whose people he had so much to give. Another link between

Nana with my mother and four cousins about 1933. The scene is Clogorrow, Athy, and the child nearest camera is Katherine Moloney who married Patrick Kavanagh in 1967. Left is Sheila Maher and right is Johnny Maher.

Karin and John was a shared admiration for the German language and culture. And once they made together the harsh pilgrimage to Lough Derg. John did his doctorate in jurisprudence at Heidelberg, where Karin and I looked him up during our honeymoon.

There was also Garret FitzGerald, still contributing his wisdom in the columns of *The Irish Times.* For nine years I edited the *Irish Times Review and Annual,* most of which was contributed by Garret. He had left Aer Lingus for the Economist Intelligence Unit and then, in tandem with (Mr Justice) Declan Costello entered politics in the cause of the "Just Society", an egalitarian document representing the views of the liberal wing of Fine Gael. I think I can safely say that for the whole nine years (1961-1970) we worked together at this end-of-year task, Garret's fee was 75 guineas. He never pushed for more and it was not in the nature of newspaper editors to offer increases. It is a pity that his vast knowledge of economics, domestic politics and foreign affairs was not enough to fend off the spendthrift tendencies of his Labour partners and give us the fiscal rectitude we needed in the 1980s when he was Taoiseach. In a note congratulating Garret on his appointment as Minister for Foreign Affairs in 1973, I half-joking whole earnestly credited him with being the

Sheila with Jim at the Coal Harbour, Dun Laoghaire in 1958.

originator of the European Union. In his reply he said: "I am quite prepared to settle for our having jointly invented the Common Market. After a year or so commuting backwards and forwards to Brussels, Luxembourg and Strasbourg I shall probably regret that we ever did invent it!".

Aedine (left) with Karin, me and my parents at Kristin's First Holy Communion, Donnybrook, 1963.

Liam Cosgrave I met only once or twice. At a lunch with Frank O'Reilly of Powers' distillery, I was surprised by Cosgrave's wit and humour and charm. Perhaps he is the kind of person who finds it hard to live under the shade of a famous father and blossoms only in small groups of people. His seeming aloofness was what Pat Lindsay of Fine Gael was alluding to in the well-known if apocryphal story he told of the fall of a Government. Cosgrave and Lindsay were driving towards Phoenix Park to hand in their seals of office to the President. Across the Liffey Cosgrave saw the Irish House. "What's that?", he asked Pat. "That's a public house, Liam", said Pat. "Hm", said Cosgrave, "I've never been in a public house". "That's why", said Pat, "we're handing in these bloody seals".

Richie Ryan was the closest I came to having a personal friend in a Fine Gael Ministry. Karin and I and later Jenny were New Year visitors to Richie and Mairéad's house for many years and it was to Richie that I appealed when he was Minister for Finance in 1973. As I tell the story in my book "God's Architect" [40], I wrote in 1973 asking him to meet my father-in-law, Raymond McGrath, when Raymond seemed to be losing the battle to have his *magnum opus*, the Kennedy Memorial Concert Hall, realised. Richie did meet McGrath, but in the end it was Richie who presided over the Government's decision to axe McGrath's ten years of work, and to build on the Earlsfort Terrace site a much reduced structure designed by Michael O'Doherty. Michael is now Raymond's successor as Principal Architect of the Office of Public Works.

Justin Keating was probably the only Labour Minister whose company I enjoyed. His father, Seán Keating the painter, was a protégé of William Orpen's and President of the Royal Hibernian Academy for twelve years. My parents knew Keating and his wife quite well. Keating painted a distinguished series of socialist realist canvases depicting the development of the Electricity Supply Board with the emphasis on the Shannon Hydro-electric Scheme. His son Justin, who was married to Loretta Wine of the well-known antique shop on Grafton Street, was Minister for Industry and Commerce in Cosgrave's Government of 1973 to 1977. Justin's aunt was Mary Frances Keating, the well-known and well-loved cookery writer for the *Sunday Independent* and, more importantly for me, the wife of Alec Newman, my pedantic Editor. Mary's loving heroism on the home front is not for this book, but it should be mentioned.

I want to leave my relationships with members of the Lemass, Lynch and Haughey cabinets to a later chapter, except to say that the 1960s formed my closest embrace with the State which has always been good to me.

The Irish House, Winetavern Street, drawn by Raymond McGrath, PRHA, for The Bell of August 1941. The pub is long demolished.

CHAPTER 14

SMYLLIE'S BROTHER

In the Spring of 1954, the *Sunday Independent* was invited by Aer Lingus to sent a representative to Lourdes on the airline's inaugural flight to that popular place of pilgrimage. Nobody else had a passport, so I was chosen *faute de mieux*. Led by J.F. (Jerry) Dempsey, the general manager, we took off in a Douglas DC3, the workhorse of the western world's airlines since 1932. It took 5 1/2 hours to reach Tarbes, still a grass strip. And we had to refuel at Dinard, where the mayor gave us a welcome that gave a new meaning to the word refuel.

The sub-editors' room in The Irish Times, about 1955. This is the room that was used in Joe Strick's movie about Leopold Bloom's visit to the Irish Independent in 1904. From left, sitting: Noel Fee, Donald Symllie, J.R. Molloy, Freddie Fox, Seamus Laverty, Bill Crampton, Dick Murphy and Jim Murphy. From left, standing: Michael Devine, Donal O'Donovan, Dermot Ashmore and Charlie Sullivan, the teaboy. Three, possibly four, are alive.

Our host on the plane and throughout was David Hayes, equally famous as Aer Lingus' public relations officer and author of "The Foley Family", a long-running serial on Radio Éireann. David it was who said of me that I got "blotto at the grotto". Of the hundreds of junkets I have been on since then, that trip to Lourdes was the booziest. It happened on 7 May 1954, a sad time for the French who that day lost Indo-China. A perfect excuse for Jack Jones of the *Irish Press* and myself to crawl around every pub in Lourdes. Dien Bien Phu where the last stand was made, is engraved on my memory, as is the reprimand I got from the Editor afterwards. I had been given £5 expenses and had such a task composing the items on my sheet that I had to resort to: "To one processional candle: five shillings". I didn't even see the procession, never mind buy a candle.

"That", said Hector Legge, "is contemptible". Dick Murphy helped me to write the story, but it was pathetic, and I found myself unable to telephone Karin to announce my return. I was incoherent.

Through a sub-editor named Tim O'Shea, I began to get casual sub-editing work on *The Irish Times*. By July, I was offered a permanent job by the chief sub-editor, Donald Smyllie. I left the *Sunday Independent* for a very different

At the opening of the refurbished lounge of the Pearl Bar, Fleet Street. From left: Alec McCabe (Alasdair Mac Cába), founder of the Educational Building Society; District Justice Donagh MacDonagh the poet and playwright; his wife Nuala (née Smith) and myself, July 1961. Alec McCabe was interned in the Emergency for his pro-German opinions, one of the very few Fine Gael supporters to have been so treated.

environment, so well described by Tony Gray in "Mr Smyllie, Sir"[41] and Charlie Orr in "Splash!"[42] that I shall resist the temptation to recount the agony and the ecstasy of life at that extraordinary newspaper. I can think of three further books, by Brian Inglis, Lionel (Bill) Fleming and Patrick Campbell, that tell the tale of R.M. Smyllie, so I can confine myself to my own experience in Fleet Street.

Richie Ryan

One evening over a quiet pint Donald Smyllie told me an extraordinary story. Before his wartime service in Burma, Donald was attached to a special airborne unit based in Troon, Scotland. Their normal work was sending agents by glider into France and retrieving them after their mission by night appointment at sea. Sometime in 1942, the unit got orders to kidnap Henning Thomsen, the counsellor at the German Legation in neutral Dublin. Smyllie and his armed party, operating a boat small enough to get under the coastal defences at Dún Laoghaire, were to force their way into the Minister's residence at nearby Monkstown. They were to take Thomsen down to Sandycove and use the same boat to carry him to the Welsh coast. There he would be easily apprehended and put away for the duration of the war. In this way, without overt interference in the Irish policy of neutrality, the leading Nazi in wartime Ireland would neatly be removed. (The German Minister, Dr. Eduard Hempel, was formally a Nazi Party member, but I, believe, had no part in espionage or destabilising de Valera's government).

R.M. Smyllie, by Robert Pyke
Courtesy of the National Gallery of Ireland.

Donald Smyllie first was sent to reconnoitre. He went initially to Westmoreland Street to see his brother Bertie, Editor of *The Irish Times.* Under the seal of Masonic secrecy, he sought Bertie's advice and help. The Editor, though he loved the people and language

George Leitch "snoozing" at the feet of the great Editor, R.M. Smyllie, in the lounge of the Pearl Bar about 1953. On Smyllie's right, head towards God, is Kevin Collins. From the left are Tony Gray, George Burrows (hard to see); Alan (Monty) Montgomery, Cathal O'Shannon, Edgar Brennan, Matt Farrell, Michael McInerney, Des O'Leary and Tony Kelly. In front of Tony is Dermot Barry, who succeeded George as Art Editor.

of the Germany that had interned him at Ruhleben twenty-five years earlier, was a sworn enemy of Nazism (he would have used a favourite word "pernicious"). He was quite disturbed by the proposal his brother brought. "Do not attempt such a foolhardy enterprise", he warned. "It could only end in the death of an Irish policeman". The mission was aborted.

The famous Editor died about two months after I joined. I saw him once in the office, a glimpse of God for which I was grateful. The perception I had of the Editor was that of a man who had brought the paper from the true-blue Unionism of John Healy's long reign (1907 to 1934) to a place in the mainstream of national life. His famous circle of friends wrote much of the paper as contributors. His own office was staffed mainly by very talented graduates of Trinity College, Dublin. Tony Gray, not a graduate, wrote "Mr. Smyllie, Sir", and left for the *Daily Mirror* in 1959. Alec Newman, who succeeded Smyllie in 1954, was eventually and inevitably fired seven years later. Bruce Williamson was literary editor when from Blackrock College I submitted my first poem to *The Irish Times*. On the rejection slip he had scribbled "I am sorry that it couldn't be a cheque. Don't be discouraged, however. I think your poem is rich with promise. Good Luck". I had imagined a greybeard of great authority and was amazed to find that Bruce was 24 in 1946, and a gentle lovable man who unfortunately chose to walk out in sympathy with Newman. The sad procession was augmented by Marion Fitzgerald, the editorial secretary who later married

Brian Fallon, now the paper's Chief Critic.

Jack White should have succeeded Smyllie, but office politics and particularly Alec Newman's insecurity (he used to call White "Jacksie" deliberately and to his face) attracted Jack to the new world of television in 1961. Jack's leading article on the dropping of the atomic bomb on Hiroshima in August 1945 is still remembered as a masterpiece of compassion, succinctness and horror. He also wrote novels and plays, and made a distinctive mark on television. Jack's departure for Montrose resolved the board's difficulties and they promptly sacked Alec. His successor was the news editor, Alan Montgomery, who after less than three years was lured to Guinness's to replace Leslie Luke. Alan (most people called him Monty, but I stuck to his given name) was self-selected. He had been asked to chair the interview board and suddenly realised that the company was offering 64 per cent more than he had as Editor.

Tony Gray lists the people who were not at Smyllie's funeral. Certainly one would have expected to see the President, Seán T. Ó Ceallaigh; the Taoiseach, John A. Costello, and the Leader of the Opposition, Éamon de Valera, who sent Michael Yeats, son of the poet, to represent him. But Gray does not say why they were not there. The reason was a Church law that forbade Catholics under pain of mortal sin to attend Protestant services, so the State

Seamus Kelly, who wrote the Quidnunc column and was the Irish Times Drama Critic for many years. Like many others, I was ambivalent about Seamus, who could use his tongue to excoriate. By Robert Pyke. Courtesy of the National Gallery of Ireland.

compromised by sending representatives. I went with my uncle Dan O'Donovan to the Scots Presbyterian Church in Abbey Street. Dan was back in the Department of Social Welfare and the two of us took our places and sang the hymns we knew. But a large gathering of Catholics stayed outside on the street, ready to follow the coffin after the service, but unwilling to risk the ire of the Archbishop of Dublin, John Charles McQuaid by taking part in the service.

Alec Newman and Bruce Williamson decided about this time to pillory Dr. McQuaid. Smyllie and the Archbishop had had an amicable relationship through the years. It culminated in an annual dinner at the Archbishop's house. Dr McQuaid's brother Matt was the sales manager for McEntaggart's of Percy

Place, the agents for the Standard motor-car. The badge of the Standard was a Union Jack and Smyllie took great pleasure in teasing the Archbishop about his choice of flag.

Things changed when Smyllie died. *The Irish Times* began a vendetta against McQuaid for his refusal to say a Votive Mass to mark the Dublin Theatre Festival on the grounds that he did not approve of the moral tone of some of the plays on offer.

Other targets of these campaigning journalists were the Fethard-on-Sea controversy and the appointment of Scott McLeod as American Ambassador to Ireland. "Scottie" was alleged to have hounded an American Communist to his death in Cairo. Details are hazy in my mind, but the campaign helped to have McLeod recalled and soon to die.

Terence White, the much-loved yet waspish Literary Editor. By Robert Pyke. Courtesy of the National Gallery of Ireland.

I found this pioneering work exciting and intoxicating. I did not know how intoxicated the authors were, but as I moved into their inner sanctum I began to see and participate in the lethal effects of alcohol on the liberal ethic.

In 1957 I was three years into my *Irish Times* life as a sub-editor. *The Irish Times* was quite different from *The Irish Independent* in many ways, one of the more important being that the Independent had a leader writers' room staffed by four journalists whose main task was to produce leading articles. They also acted as an embryonic features department and as literary editors. These men - always men then - included Ben Kiely for a while but more durably Tom O'Donnell, a former Editor of the *Sunday;* Paddy Glendon, the art critic, (now Professor) Gerry Quinn, Frank D'Arcy, Paddy Bourke, S.C., his son Marcus the writer; Louis McRedmond who became Editor, and Rory O'Hanlon, the paper's Irish language expert, later a controversial High Court judge. There was a strong Bar Library bias in that chamber. In *The Irish Times,* the Editor, his deputy, the features editor and the literary editor, as well as one or two editorial assistants, were expected to contribute leading articles on what were seen as their fields of expertise.

Martin Sheridan was an editorial assistant who was offered the job of public relations officer to Córas Tráchtála, the Irish Export Board. He went with alacrity and carved himself a fine career. I was amazed when Donald Smyllie suggested that I should apply for his job.

"Me?", I said. "I couldn't write a leader to save my life".

"Have a go", said Donald. "It can't do any harm".

So I fearfully approached Alec Newman, who asked me to write a piece on the British National Health Service as a test. Making use of Whitaker's Almanack, I produced an article for the Editor.

"I was going to give you a week's trial", said Alec, "but now there is no need". I was to join the élite, the club that gave me in Stanley Baldwin's famous phrase, "power without responsibility, the prerogative of the harlot through the ages".

I exercised that power without responsibility for the next thirteen years. On at least one occasion, I wrote all three leaders, but normally the third was the "pup" leader, usually a comic comment on a strange news story. In my time, these were contributed, equally brilliantly, by Alec Reid, R.B.D. French, both lecturers at Trinity College, or by Marion Fitzgerald, our editorial secretary, who was weaned on pups and went on to much more substantial journalism.

One night Alec looked at my white face and asked where I had been. "I have been vomiting pints", I told him.

"Be thankful Donal", said the Editor, "that you can still get sick. The time will come when you will no longer be able to throw up". He was right.

On another night I was acting Editor when Seán MacBride came in. Ten minutes later, we had a visit from Major Tom McDowell, the managing director. I introduced Seán by saying: "This is Major McDowell, our new hatchet man".

Things were changing again. Alec and Bruce were gone. Terence de Vere White replaced Jack White as our literary editor and though books had replaced the law as his domain, he was expected to write an appropriate leader like the rest of us. Alan Montgomery did not write. He edited the paper for three years but wrote no leaders. When he assumed the editorial chair for the first time, in late 1961, I sat opposite him and asked: "What are we writing about tonight?"

"What makes you think you are writing at all?", he replied. He was suspicious of me as a relic of the *ancien régime*, thinking perhaps that I had stayed on as the observer for those who had departed. But he soon realised that he had nobody else, and our hostility turned into a warm friendship that lasted to his death in 1996 at 84. I do remember Alan's receiving a letter from Archbishop McQuaid. "Dear Mr. Montgomery", he wrote, "I should like to congratulate you on your appointment as Editor of *The Irish Times,* which I read of in the *Daily Telegraph*". I thought this comic olive branch should be seized and suggested that Monty should ask the Archbishop to tea. Alan thought otherwise, so the feud persisted.

Dick Gamble I drank with a lot, our favourite day being Sunday when we would take our wives to lunch in the Dolphin, drink all afternoon and turn up drunk for work. Sometimes we were not up to it. Dick, who doubled as motoring correspondent, had a beautiful wife Jean, who is now Mrs. Hugh Crawford.

Fergus Pyle joined us at the watershed. He was on a month's trial when Alec was fired. He soon became features editor after me and in the 1970s was Editor for a while. He died in 1997 when he was Chief Leader Writer, bringing his lively, accurate and cosmopolitan style to his writing. Fergus, who was only 62, had more international experience than anybody on the paper. His sister Hilary is the well-known art historian and biographer of Jack B. Yeats.

CHAPTER 15

LEITCH OF INDIA

Double jobbing was common practice in Dublin newspapers. Pay was low, although the senior reporter's rate had more than doubled in 1947 when the new and enlightened Labour Court (a year old) raised the rate from four guineas to nine, a feat for which Michael Rooney, later Editor of the *Irish Independent*, was given a gold watch by a grateful press.

Michael, a feisty Northerner, was the Institute of Journalists' representative on the negotiating team, and he and Tom O'Donnell, late of the *Sunday Independent*, pressed me to go for the presidency of the Institute in 1959. I was

My stag party at 28 Upper Fitzwilliam Street. From left: Donald Smyllie, Gerry O Donovan, Bill Crampton, myself, Michael Devine and Dick Murphy. October 1954. Picture taken by George Leitch of The Irish Times.

drunk during most of the conference at Southend-on-Sea and did nothing to further my candidacy. I remember that Malta and Nigeria voted for me. Belfast, Glasgow and Edinburgh pledged their votes to me but I later found that they placed their Protestant or Masonic preference elsewhere. We had an enjoyable day trip to Ostend by plane and I made a connection that got me proposed and accepted as a member of the Royal Commonwealth Society. It was the nearest I could get to membership of a London club and its simple rooms were both reasonable and central. I used the mailboat for council meetings of the Institute, but it was clear that the National Union of Journalists was winning the membership battle. Soon, the NUJ operated a closed shop in Ireland and the Institute broke up, though not before I gained valuable experience as a member of the National Council for the Training of Journalists. The scene is very different today, when aspiring journalists have several colleges to choose from. What they miss is the provincial paper experience that supplied the Dublin papers with able reporters and sub-editors for perhaps 150 years.

I had no such training, but I did double-job on the new *Evening Press* in 1954, when Douglas Gageby was the founding Editor. Douglas is the greatest journalist this country has produced. He is a Belfast Protestant who was born in Dublin and wears the mantle of Wolfe Tone. After a distinguished career at Trinity College, he joined the Army as a private in 1939; rose to captain in G2

My supplement on India comes off the Irish Times press on 26 January 1970. Left: Edwin Dunning, advertising display manager; Anthony G. Meneses, Ambassador of India, and myself.

(Military Intelligence) under the legendary Colonel Dan Bryan, and joined the *Irish Press* immediately after the war. He wrote a remarkable series of articles on post-war Germany and by 1949 had been made assistant editor of the new *Sunday Press*, edited by Colonel Matt Feehan and inspired by Seán Lemass to "knock the guts out of the *Sunday Independent*".[43]

A year later, Seán MacBride's baby, the Irish News Agency, was born, and Gageby was its second editor. The managing director was Conor Cruise O'Brien of the Department of External Affairs. A galaxy of talent was attracted to the INA, which was designed to pierce the Green Curtain that was perceived to surround Ireland. Between conflicts of interest in the Dublin newspaper world and lack of interest on the part of the greater world outside, the agency never took off as a source of managed news and when de Valera came back to power in 1957, it was closed down. It had paid well and helped to boost journalists' salaries all round.

Then came the *Evening Press*. Launched in September 1954, it was as great a success as the *Sunday Press* had been, and Gageby, later to boost the circulation of *The Irish Times* from 30,000-plus to three times that figure, was its Editor. In the sub-editors' room, the acerbic John O'Donovan reigned supreme, or thought he did. Bill Crampton and I, both double jobbing, were not above spiking any story that we did not like, and John never noticed. But he was a superb music critic, a great writer of historical features (under the pen-name Andrew Marsh), a witty talker and a non-smoking teetotal vegetarian. His letters programme "Dear Sir or Madam" ran on Radio Éireann for years. For some of those years he was assisted by Jenny McGrath Kinnane, who became my wife in 1968 and will loom large in later pages.

Andrew Stuart was the resident Scot - every newspaper had a Scot. In the White Horse one day, Andy told me the story of the four leader-writers on *The Times* of London. One night only one turned up. The Editor was in despair. Each leader-writer was entitled to a bottle of port, so the survivor said he would write all four editorials if he got all four bottles of port. Agreed. Two hours later, the Editor found him slumped over the desk, the bottles empty and in his typewriter a sheet of paper on which he had managed to write: "Moreover,".

As a source of extra income, the *Evening Press* was fine, but I was soon attracted to the *Irish Farmers' Journal,* recently bought over by Michael Dillon and Paddy O'Keeffe. Paddy was the Editor, a small, stocky, aggressive and dynamic Fermoy man who has become a power in the business world. Noel Fee, the assistant chief sub-editor in *The Irish Times*, told me there was sub-editing work there - there being Earlsfort Terrace in those days and Noel himself being a double jobber. Maeve O'Shea (later Walsh) was O'Keeffe's secretary and a mighty drinker. We had two watering holes, both unlikely. Behind us was Harcourt Street Station which until Todd Andrews closed it in 1959 had its own bar with its own licensing laws. And beside us was the RAF Club, where there was even less risk of a garda raid. There too was George Leitch, the chief photographer of *The Irish Times* and the greatest male friend I have had.

George Leitch was born in 14 Goldsmith Street, Phibsborough, Dublin, in 1899. Early on, he was given a stuffed bear to play with. You couldn't call it a Teddy bear because George was given it just after Theodore Roosevelt first became President of the United States and before bears were named after him. The bear, one ear missing and foot pads worn, now belongs to my daughter Síofra.

George and Donald Smyllie, my other good friend of those times, told me soon after I joined them that they had been suspicious of me at first because they thought I was a German fascist through my wife. I couldn't blame them. George had served in the Royal Flying Corps which in 1918 became the Royal Air Force; and Donald had seen distinguished service in Burma in the Second World War. They had no love for Germans.

One of the British officers in the Younghusband expedition was George's father. Colonel (later Sir) F.E. Younghusband was sent with an armed escort provided by the Vicerory of India, Lord Curzon, to replace diplomacy by force in Britain's dealings with the Dalai Lama. Younghusband reached Lhasa after some severe fighting in August 1904. The Dalai Lama fled and peace was made in treaties with Tibet, China, Russia and Sikkim. That troubled country has a long history of Chinese invasions and annexations, a history that George's father, Major Leitch, imparted to him in the years he spent in the Indian Army. The saga of Tibet, as we know, is not ended, as Frank Aiken pointed up so sharply in the UN when he was Minister for External Affairs in 1959, the year the Dalai Lama fled from Chinese conquerors.

George was ten when he discovered his mother in bed with another officer. He had to appear in court to testify to her adultery, an event that left a deep scar. He joined *The Irish Times* in 1922 as the paper's first and for a few years only photographer and he became famous for his devilment as much as for his work. His only enemy that I know of was Joe Cashman, the Cork photographer whose pictorial record of the blasting of Dublin during the Troubles has given him a lasting renown. Joe, whom I had the pleasure of knowing, was the man who took the celebrated photograph of Jim Larkin dressed as a priest and addressing the crowd from the balcony during the 1913 lockout. I suppose George was flying for king and country. And enjoying himself doing it.

George's marriage was no happier than mine and he knew, when Karin died, that I would marry again. With deep insight and great glee, he vetted and vetoed several women to whom I introduced him. I am glad to say that he thoroughly approved of Jenny. In fact they became fast friends and we shared the sorrow of his passing in 1981.

George Patrick Leitch as he leaves for the Irish rugby team's tour of New Zealand in 1976

George ended his days in the Old Men's Home for Reduced Citizens of Dublin, Northbrook Road. The matron was Carrie Greenham and as proof that George had the secret of eternal youth they entered into a warm relationship. "Prayer, fasting and self-denial" was George's ideal. He never practised what he preached, though he watched the last years of my alcoholic drinking with deep concern, and matching joy when I stopped.

CHAPTER 16

DEATH IN PETRA

At John Kelly's wedding to Delphine Dudley in 1961, a memorable day in the sun at the Dudleys' place near Mallow, a strange rivalry was demonstrated. The contestants were Patrick Gallagher, a barrister, journalist and booklover, now alas dead, and Ronan Keane now a member of the Supreme Court and a distinguished writer on legal matters. The prize was a Miss Terry O'Donnell, soon to be a journalist. Paddy lost and Terry married Ronan.

The rivalry never developed into enmity. When Paddy died, Ronan wrote an unusually warm appreciation in *The Irish Times*. He described Paddy as "that rare person in a county over-populated with carefully constructed 'characters', a genuine eccentric". Paddy was:

> . . . One of a gifted generation who graduated from UCD in the late 1940s and early 1950s, many of whom became and remained friends . . .It was of course the old world of Earlsfort Terrace and Leeson Street, the pubs and coffee-shops, the art galleries, theatres and cinemas, gone forever with the move to the concrete wastes of Belfield . . .

Terry and Ronan's was a stormy relationship, not made harmonious by Terry's forceful personality and wayward behaviour. She was charming, beautiful and funny, critical and generous, the Lady Lavery of modern Ireland. She probably still is all those things, but I have not seen her for many years, so I don't know. She always wanted to be famous, and I did a little to help her by appointing her Fashion Correspondent of *The Irish Times* in the 1960s. We were for some years special friends, but not sexually intimate. It was about 1975 that I wrote a piece of whimsy about her which went in part:

The death took place in Petra yesterday of Mrs. Terry Keane. She was believed to be four score years and ten - the age at which she had always promised to die. World reaction was instant. The Dow Jones average dropped to the lowest level since the Sino-Japanese war and on the commodity market all copper futures became pasts.

In Peiping, Chairman Mao Tse-tung brightened perceptibly, and in Chappaquidick President Edward Kennedy became quite ill. Shops closed for two days along the Wailing Wall of Jerusalem and the Taoiseach, Mr.Haughey, travelled to Kiltimagh to pay tribute to his ancestors.

On the Al-hamra in Beyrouth, the price of shoes and Irish Coffee rose to a new high in anticipation of the arrival of a dozen international jet-setters on a pre-funeral shopping spree.

From his palace in Amman the Hashemite King of Jordan proclaimed a national day of mourning for the woman he had hoped to present with an assortment of Holy Places.

In Dublin, Ireland, of which Mrs. Keane had been inordinately fond, an ard-fheis of pet dogs and politicians' wives unleashed the bitches, causing a high-decibel noise that could be heard by the Taoiseach who by this time had arrived in the suburbs of Kiltimagh complete with torchlight procession.

A jubilant Mr. Keane made immediate plans to drop the entire Bar in the Liffey and settle in the South of France.

Mrs Keane, who was as well known for her literary allusions as for her other exploits, left four children (usually in good health).

Tomorrow all four will go on a shopping trip to Dublin to buy suitable rosary beads, which they will send by Army despatch riders to the Rose Red City. After the funeral, the children will have a word to say to the   Shahanshah of Persia, in whose gem-encrusted arms the late Mrs Keane passed away.

As she expressed a final sigh, Mrs. Keane was heard to say: "Of course darling, I had never considered dying anywhere but in Petra . . ."

While there is and must be a certain amount of code in this (and more in the rest of it), it is worth recording that the piece was written at least four years before Charles J. Haughey became Taoiseach. He was in the period of political exile imposed on him after the Arms Trial of 1970. It was a slow climb back although he had been found not guilty of conspiring to import arms. But his lifestyle was not damaged.

When I heard of his arrest I went into shock. I rang Dick Walsh of *The Irish Times* and asked him what could possibly have motivated Haughey to get involved in this way in the Northern Troubles. I expected him to say something like, " He was getting 10 percent on the shipment"; but Dick's reply was: "Pure patriotism". Still dismayed, and feeling betrayed by a friend and a senior Minister, I drove my car into the back of a Fiat 850 at Cabinteely, and as the subsequent trial proceeded, I decided not to speak to Charlie again.

But a couple of years later, when I was drinking in the Royal Hibernian Hotel (I had an account there for a while until I considered that there were other uses for money than high living in the Lafayette Restaurant, even though it was Bank of Ireland's money), Terry Keane brought me over to her table, where Charlie sat. I had no choice short of downright rudeness but to shake hands.

Soon I was a member of the circle that included Ray MacSharry, who day after day sat patiently beside Haughey and nursed his Club Orange. The rest of us drank Bullshots. A Bullshot was a cocktail made of consommé and vodka. It was nearly as lethal as the Martinis that Seán MacBride used to make and serve at Roebuck House on a Sunday morning. At Roebuck we said that Seán passed the cork of the Martini bottle over the gin.

In spite of the regularity with which we met in the 1970s, my attraction to Haughey was different in kind from my feeling for him in the 1960s. For one thing, I had joined Fianna Fáil in 1971 to shore up the support for Jack Lynch in North Wicklow. I no longer held a position which made me useful to Haughey. I had left *The Irish Times* five months before the Arms Trial to become public relations manager of the Bank of Ireland.

CHAPTER 17

THE GENTLEMEN'S STRIKE

This is the hardest part of my story to write. I could leave it out or tone it down. Or I could tell most of the truth. Not the whole truth because, in the first place, it might hurt people and secondly, I might invite the wrath of a mighty institution.

Towards the end of 1969, I got a telephone call from Donal Shemus Allingham Carroll, Governor of the Bank of Ireland. Would I, he wanted to know, be interested in setting up a public relations department in the bank? He arranged a lunch in the Intercontinental Hotel. He did not attend. I was the guest of Raffe Roberts, marketing manager, and Pat Elliott, personnel director, and we were to discuss terms and conditions. I should have asked where Carroll was: his absence was a portent.

My first question was: Why am I sitting down with two Englishmen? Raffe replied: "You'd better answer that, Pat". Elliott told me they had scoured the two islands and there was nobody better to be found than Raffe Roberts. As for himself, he had some kind of Dublin connection.

They were offering £3,500 plus car loan at 4% and house loan at 3%. In *The Irish Times* I was on £2,750, I had just got a staff car and I was paying 9% for my mortgage. Douglas Gageby was not sorry to see me go but he did say I should hold out for £4,000. My self-confidence was low because I had been moved sideways to the post of features manager and especially because my new wife Jenny was in St. Patrick's Hospital suffering from a very severe depression.

My swansong was a twelve page supplement on Ireland and India. I was dealing with a Goan named Tony Meneses, Ambassador of India. Indira Gandhi and Jack Lynch wrote the front page between them: the other eleven pages I wrote myself as the product of a magical trip to New Delhi, Bombay, Bangalore and Madras. I had as guide a third secretary from Foreign Affairs named Shrin Rai Singh, a man of gentle nature and unhappy soul. He was bullied by his senior in Delhi, was married to a double of Anna Manahan, was not a supporter of the Congress Party, and killed himself a couple of years later. He was an informed and sensitive guide on my journey, which began with a reception at the equivalent of Iveagh House.

I got in touch with Raj Tandon, the courtly predecessor of Tony Meneses in Dublin and then retired to a job with Binny's the textile giants. Raj set up a party for me at the Delhi Gymkhana Club for the coming Sunday. In the meanwhile, he said, I simply must see the Taj Mahal by moonlight. A delightful prospect, I thought, until Mr Rai Singh said on Friday that there was just a chance of meeting the President of India on Saturday morning. He left the choice to me, and I chose President V.V. Giri because I knew he had been a student at the College of Surgeons in 1916 and had been friendly with Patrick Pearse and James Connolly.

I made the right choice and really enjoyed my visit to the President's office in the Government Buildings designed by Lutyens. Next evening at the club, the first question was how had I enjoyed the visit to Agra. I told Raj I had had a glorious opportunity of meeting his President. He was aghast. "Not *that* little man!" he almost shouted and was supported by the Editors of the *Times of India* and the *Statesman* and a host of distinguished guests. I felt as though I were telling a dinner party at the Kildare Street Club that I had visited Seán T. Ó Ceallaigh at Áras an Uachtaráin in preference to having dinner with the Earl of Rosse at Birr Castle.

The supplement was a success. Not a huge commercial profit-maker, but the Indian Government liked it. One of the factories I was shown made telephone equipment and I asked the management about a recent order from Plessey in Ireland worth £200,000. "Oh that", the director said. "We make sophisticated products for places such as Kenya. The Irish order is being executed out in the back - it's for last -generation crossbar equipment". I had no comment to make.

In February 1970 I began the Bank of Ireland job, totally ignorant of how banks were structured. I didn't know that if you called yourself Public Relations Manager, that made you a bank manager. That determined the size of your desk, your ashtray, your chair. Rank determined whether you had lunch in the Directors' or the Executive dining room or the staff canteen, where I ate. I could invite guests to the private dining rooms on the top floor where the food was haute cuisine, but I could not know that I was seen as an outsider. Almost everybody had joined the bank at eighteen and could look forward to retirement at 65 on a pension of two-thirds of salary.

I could not have chosen a worse time to join the bank.

The Irish Bank Officials' Association, led by the fiery John Titterington, was coming to the boil. Pay and conditions were inadequate, but public sympathy was lacking. First, the perception was that bank officials led sheltered, privileged lives of considerable affluence; and secondly the IBOA was not a member of the Irish Congress of Trade Unions, its members regarding themselves as a cut above the working man.

I was introduced to the regional managers by Ian Morrison, the Chief Executive of the Bank of Ireland and a formidable figure. I did not impress the meeting. I was timid where I should have been brash; hesitant where I should have displayed a command of my communications skills. I could blame Jenny's illness, but it was more than that. Colonel Osborne had seen that I was no salesman in 1950: Ian Morrison was witnessing the same phenomenon twenty years on.

The IBOA strike of May 1970 was to endure for six months and to become a subject of worldwide interest and amusement. How could a country survive without its banks? The answer was: very nicely thank you. The supermarkets devised means of lodging their vast volumes of cash. Alternative financial institutions developed emergency clearing facilities and subsidiary firms in the money market grew wings. International payments were made by devious means. Cheques were by and large honoured and new unofficial chequebooks were printed. The clearing system was suspended, but other ways were found, and many bank officials either took extended holidays or went to work elsewhere.

The banks themselves, in the form of the Banks Staff Relations Committee, had to answer questions and deal with the media in an open way that was alien to their secretive natures. Because most of their staff - there were a few "exempted" officials at management level - were on the street, they had no spokesman except me, the only non-member of the IBOA, the only member of the National Union of Journalists.

I was all they had for a few months, until they recruited Joe Dillon of Arrow Advertising to supplement (replace?) my efforts. I was elevated to strategy meetings of the Bank of Ireland and of all the four Associated Banks. They were not pretty sights.

Ned Gray, tragically killed in the Staines air disaster of 1972, conducted the Banks' campaign. He was director-general of the Confederation of Irish Industry and was seconded to act as the bosses' man. He knew the banking industry well, having worked through a shorter dispute in 1966.

Ned was one of those grand people that a long life throws up. He was honourable, lively, even funny. He was a straight talker who could see the whole picture. As I write, I use a bronze paper weight that Ned gave me, to prevent these pages from blowing away in the wind.

Ned had one fault: a fierce and sudden temper. He was aware of it and went to church most mornings to ask God for help with it. I recall being told of one late night meeting at which he almost came to blows with Ian Morrison over strategy. He called Morrison " a dirty black Scotch Protestant bastard", a remark which puzzled Morrison. Next day, Morrison was still puzzled. He asked me: "What did Ned mean? We grew up almost side by side in Clontarf".

The trouble was that by August, Morrison and some of the other bank leaders wanted to settle with the staff and get back to normal work. Ned Gray and Joe Gilroy, the Chief General Manager of the Bank of Ireland, were determined, with others, to see the fight through to the end. One day Ned and Joe, Jeff McDonnell and I had a lunch meeting in a private room in the Intercontinental Hotel. Jeff was General Manager East and had been in the Army with Joe. After a general survey of the state of play, Jeff said to Joe: "The difference between you and me, Joe, is that we're both bolloxes, but I know it".

For those two men, just turned fifty, the end of the strike brought sadness. Joe Gilroy was quietly retired - no loss of salary, no deprivation of Mércèdes, just go. Joe assumed that Jeff would succeed him, rang Jeff from Hume House to College Green, and told him he was on. Jeff presented himself to Morrison, was asked what he was doing there, retired with his tail between his legs and was soon made Director of Institutional Relations with an office on the directors' floor, a telephone, a table and an unquestioned expense account to go to Brussels or wherever he liked, but no work to do. The General Manager West, Paddy Heffernan, got Joe's job, and within a couple of years Joe Gilroy was dead.

I watched all this with grim amusement. In Joe Gilroy's case, I asked Brendan O'Regan whether he could find something useful for Joe to do because I knew that enforced idleness would destroy him. O'Regan was the Father of Shannon, the son of a hotelier who owned the Old Ground in Ennis. He began a meteoric career by ferrying food from the Old Ground to the flying boat base at Foynes during the Second World War, when Foynes was host to almost every V.I.P. crossing the Atlantic. When Shannon Airport opened in 1945, O'Regan became Catering Comptroller and on up to the top in what became the Shannon Free Airport Development Company, later Shannon Development.

One of the brightest stars in Seán Lemass's firmament, he not only spewed out ideas: he acted on them, and thus transformed County Clare and the Mid-West region into the prosperous centre of industry, tourism and agriculture that they are today. Later, he bent his energies to the development of Co-operation North, a reconciliation agency in which he tried in vain to involve me. I'm afraid I regarded it as a piece of moneyed do-goodery. Still do.

At any rate (by which I mean that I am giving more space to Brendan O'Regan than to many others because Hickey and Doherty [44] unaccountably ignore him while giving the history of SFADCO), O'Regan found a niche for Joe Gilroy. I don't remember now what it was, but I have a copy of my letter to O'Regan, addressed to Mount Henry, Killaloe:

Dear Brendan,

I have heard through the grapevine what you have done for Joe Gilroy.

You have made a new man of him. I am very very grateful.

Yours ever

Joe's wife Mary was a sister of Oliver Moylan, the owner of Ennis Cash Stores, one of the biggest firms in the town, so the Clare connection was already there. Joe himself was an Omagh man, a school friend of Benedict Kiely the novelist, also my friend

The Minister for Labour at the time of the dispute was Joe Brennan, the poll-topping T.D. for Donegal-Leitrim. Brennan requested Professor Michael P. Fogarty of the Economic and Social Research Institute to inquire into the dispute, report on it and make recommendations designed to avoid a repetition.

Fogarty reported [45] on 17 May 1971. It was a straight-talking comprehensive document of 205 pages. I would not have expected him to refer to any of the matters I have described, but I did think it distinctly odd that he did not talk to me, especially as he praises the media for its reporting of the

With Rita Childers, widow of the President, at a reception in the Hanly Centre, Dun Laoghaire in 1988

dispute. Fogarty (section 232) says:

. . . Obviously one cannot expect all the angles of the dispute to be brought into every article. Press, radio and television reports appear day by day and each report is inevitably fragmentary. But if, as I have done, one reads back through the whole file of press cuttings from the beginning of the dispute to the end, and compares this with information from other sources, one can only end by congratulating the press on the service which it has provided to the public.

The information that the media so competently gave to the public had to come from somewhere. I suggest that on the banks' side and at least until Joe Dillon appeared, that "somewhere" was me. Fogarty points out that the IBOA "had a personal, clearly identifiable leader", whereas " . . . the facelessness of the Banks' Staff Relations Committee has been a disadvantage to the banks not only - nor even primarily - during negotiations, but even more during the build-up to negotiations and the process of settling down afterwards".

I can only assume that Fogarty's failure to include me in his consultations stemmed from the division on the banks' side. After August 1970, I often found myself with a media enquiry that required a response which was elicited by me from the anti-settlement side. I had somehow become identified with the Ned Grays and the Joe Gilroys and was not being taken into the confidence of the group who wanted to resolve the dispute.

This unfortunate beginning was to mark most of my career with the Bank of Ireland. I was an outsider: I remained an outsider and in the eyes of the staff a boss's man. I can't blame the ordinary IBOA member who did not understand why I was there in the first place. In a sense I was no different from Raffe Roberts or Pat Elliott, handpicked by Donal Caroll in the mistaken belief that I was what the bank needed.

And the settlement itself? The terms gave the staff an opportunity to do as much overtime as would compensate them for the income they lost by going on strike. Professor Fogarty asks: was it worth it?

The mountain has laboured and out has come a ridiculous mouse; a plump, well-fed, mouse if you like, a pleasure for any bank official to have around the house; but still a mouse of very much the same size and shape as all the other mice generated with far less fuss and bother in a range of other occupations, public and private, which did not need a five-and-a-half months' stoppage to do it.

Paddy Heffernan, Chief General Manager of the Bank of Ireland; Charlie Haughey and Sir Robert Lowry (later Lord Lowry) Chief Justice of Northern Ireland at a horse show at Abbeville, Kinsealy about 1974. I'm in the background.

Myself, I was given a bonus of £500. I had abstained from alcohol throughout the strike and felt that I deserved a drink.

A year after I joined the bank, a deeply distressing thing happened. The advertising manager of *The Irish Times* was Brian Dawson, with whom I had worked closely towards the end of my time on the paper. Brian several times suggested lunch and I put him off. I sensed that something was wrong.

But nothing prepared me for the news that Brian had shot himself. All I could do by way of reparation for my deafness to his plea for help was to write this poem:

For Brian 22.2.1971

It was a hollow morning
The morning they planted him
And his woman wearing eyes by
    Wally Cole.

Quietly only family they planted him
After we all sang the psalm
And he would have thought it a poor production
    Organisationwise
    Or laughed.

The drill was bad, aimless even
Like his own end maybe
Or was it that we partly knew
Why he didn't use
    The telephone?

CHAPTER 18

THE TWO ERSKINES

My links with Shannon began with a flight on a DC3 in 1946. In 1957, I applied for a job in the publicity department and was interviewed by J.G. Ryan and Jack Lynch separately. I did not get the post but those two men, O'Regan's lieutenants, remind me of an anecdote about Erskine Childers, a friend and neighbour in Rathgar and Minister for Transport and Power from 1959 to 1969. Carrying that portfolio, he supervised the activities of SFADCO. One day, Childers summoned the Secretary of the Department, R.C.O'Connor, and asked him if it was true as he had been told that all the senior men in SFADCO were Blackrock College men and members of the Knights of Columbanus.

"Yes and no, Minister", replied O'Connor. "Yes they, like O'Regan, went to Blackrock. No none of them is a member of the Knights".

"That's all right", said Childers, " thank you Mr. O'Connor".

As the Secretary left the room, Childers said, "Just a minute, Mr. O'Connor. Could you tell me how you know this fact?"

"Yes Minister", said O'Connor, holding up the hand with the ring finger, "because I am a Knight myself".

By the early 1960s, I had developed my warm friendship with Shannon and Brendan O'Regan and Vincent Tobin, who died before Christmas 1996 of a serious cancer. I had a strong belief in the growth of the company and fairly frequently wrote editorials to counter the Dublin-centred bias of the

Establishment. The imbalance between East and West was obvious and the Mid-West got my support when it was needed. In return, my wife and children and I were given generous hospitality and notable gestures of warmth.

When Karin died, Brendan (known as BOR in the company) offered me a senior post in public relations. I considered his offer overnight and was surprised when he said next morning that he would have to retract it. He had been told in no uncertain terms by that part of the company that they wanted no outsider. It was embarrassing for O'Regan but it did nothing to upset our friendship.

Through Brendan and Vincent I met many people. Vincent's wife Orla, a Timon from Dublin, was endlessly kind through times of crisis and remains a true friend. Naoise (Ignatius) Cleary, the schoolmaster of Corofin, visited us up to his death. His retirement was devoted to building up the Clare Heritage Centre and for that work he received a People of the Year Award. I called to see him one morning and greeted him with a jocular "Good morning, Dr. Cleary". His face turned deep red and he answered: "How did you know that I am to get a doctorate? I only heard myself yesterday". You have to be careful what you say in jest.

These people of Clare nurtured me through bad times, though I have to say that they found my friendship/affair with Barbara Smith hard to take. About 1965, when I was swanning about Europe, going to OECD meetings in Paris for the hell of it and finding excuses to visit London, I met Barbara Smith, then international editor of *The Economist*. We were guests at a party given by John Kelly's journalist brother David. I invited her over to Ireland after Karin died, and she brought her son Adam. They stayed with Kristin and me at our small apartment in Monkstown and then I took them on a tour of the Clare and Galway countryside. There we conceived the idea of buying two acres of land at Ballymaley, near Ennis, and building a hotel. We got Bord Fáilte approval for a ten-bedroom hotel by the lake and Paddy Delany, the architectural correspondent of *The Irish Times* and a part-time music critic there as well, prepared the planning application.

This was alcoholic pie in the sky. I had no money: Barbara had a little. The land went to us for £1,760 and I asked Barbara for £500, which she gave me out of her savings for Adam's education. When the time came to pay the balance through my gentlemanly solicitor, James B. MacClancy of Ennis, I had to let the deal lapse. A fair amount of time and correspondence went on this will o' the wisp pursuit, and a lot of hardship was caused to Barbara Smith, whom I last saw in June 1968. I am not proud of that exercise in irresponsibility, which ended in

MacClancy's exasperated statement: "I cannot understand why you do not reply to my letters or telephone calls".

The site was subsequently sold for £2,100 to Clare County Council and provides a fine amenity area for the people of Ennis.

The first article I wrote in *The Irish Times* caused a storm of protest. Karin and I travelled to Sweden to stay with her brother Donal and his Dublin wife Una, living at Västerås. That was in 1955. Donal was an engineer with ASEA and Karin was pregnant with Kristin. The fourth-class dormitory on the boat from Harwich to Gothenburg was not comfortable and she swayed for the whole three weeks we were on dry land.

Time had recently published a cover story on "Sin in Sweden", so my article struck the Swedes at a sensitive point. I talked of the suicide rate, the divorce rate, free love - as we used to call promiscuity - and the welfare state. I made it quite clear that my observations were based on a limited stay: I did not mention that I had talked to the Irish Ambassador, my friend Brendan Dillon, and his wife Alice among others.

The Swedish Embassy sent a formal note of protest to the Department of External Affairs; the Ambassador asked Professor Jim Carney to prepare a reply on Sweden's behalf, and Dr. Denis Kendrick O'Donovan wrote to *The Irish Times* disclaiming any connection with the D.K. O'Donovan who had written the article. He lived in Fitzwilliam Place: I in Upper Fitzwilliam Street, so the risk of confusion and contamination was palpable.

Jim Carney, who was in the School of Celtic Studies in the Dublin Institute for Advanced Studies, was a convinced Swedophile and his rebuttal was published. The principal result for me was the formation of a close friendship with the man who was the father of Mr. Justice Paul Carney.

Jack Lynch was Minister for Education when I interviewed him for a series of profiles that Jack White asked me to do. It was the first time I had heard the phrase, "Sure I only met the scholars coming home". It reminded me of the remark made by Seán Moylan, Lynch's predecessor, who said that de Valera's appointing him Minister for Education proved that Dev had a sense of humour.

I kept no record of these profiles - just as well, says you: we're getting enough - but I do remember calling Todd Andrews "the high priest of the cult of Synge Street". Todd wasn't sure how to take that.

That was the year (1956) that Pronnséas O'Sullivan died. Two months later, Kristin was born. Pronnséas was born in 1889 in an unlikely place called Inchitaglin, Adrigole, West Cork. He was one of the Sullivan Eugenes, a nomenclature that reflected the profusion of otherwise indistinguishable O'Sullivans in that place. We know from his niece, Maureen O' Shea of Lauragh, Kenmare, that his parents had little Irish and that he was one of a family of nine.

In 1910 he began to teach in a primary school in Dublin and Aindrias Ó Muíneacháin says in Irish that at that time Pronnséas was "not reluctant" to go on his bike to Wicklow and spend the night teaching Irish there. He was a prominent member of the Five Provinces branch of the Gaelic League (known as "The Five Protestants" because of the religious persuasion of its most prominent members). Mary Spring Rice got him a job in Foynes and sent him to Kerry to find out the best place to land German guns. She was Lord Monteagle's daughter and accompanied Erskine Childers and his wife on the yacht Asgard which accomplished the Howth gun-running in 1914.

Irish was the love of Pronnséas's life, and I only add this memoir to what I have written earlier because it has not been written in English before. My account comes from Diarmuid Breathnach and Mary Murphy's splendid "Beathasnéis a Ceathair" [46].

As Kristin ceased to toddle, we tried to get herself and Erskine and Rita Childers' daughter Nessa together as little playmates in the sandpit. They took an instant scunner against each other and the days of Erskine and me being the only fathers in Rathgar to push a pram were over. Erskine, a studious serious man who was never accused of having a sense of humour, was Minister for Lands, Forestry and Fisheries at the time, fulfilling his pledge to his eponymous father to devote his life to public service.

Erskine Hamilton Childers was elected President of Ireland in 1973 and died in office two years later. He was a good friend but a man who always found it difficult to get elected. To him and to his son Erskine Barton Childers I owe a great debt of gratitude. They taught me what precision and clarity of thought were. Erskine B., who died in 1996 after a lifetime in the United Nations, chaired a radio talk show in the 1950s. At that time, the programme, "Round Table on

World Affairs" went out on Sunday mornings, when I would have a considerable hangover, but with Jack White and Kevin B. Nowlan (I can't recall anybody else), I struggled through the complexities of foreign policy under a master broadcaster. Ní fheicfimid a leithéidí arís.

CHAPTER 19

NIKOLASCHKA

The Germans became more confident as their Economic Miracle became the wonder of the world. In 1958, they organised a German Fortnight in Dublin. Karin was the secretary: I was the press agent. We lunched in Jammet's every day of the two weeks. Freddy Kolb was the embassy's cultural attaché. Freddy, who died in 1990, played a central role in the recasting of Irish-German relations after the war.

A native of Munich, he had served in the Luftwaffe and was shot down over England. His posting to Ireland in 1951 was not by any means his first visit because his aunt was married to Professor William Stockley of Cork. Another aunt, Annette Kolb, was a novelist and biographer of Mozart and Schubert. He worked with Helmut Clissmann at founding St. Kilian's School, where Kristin spent her early years. And with Pronnséas O'Sullivan he set up the Irish-German Society, to become the Goethe Institut.

Dr. Alfred Kolb, Bruno Achilles the chancellor of the embassy, and Dr. Séamus Mallon chose the superb site for the German War Cemetery at Glencree, Co. Wicklow.

I wrote an appreciation of Freddy for *The Irish Times*, an act of piety that brought back memories. In the late 1950s and early 1960s I had contributed a short weekly column to the paper. It was called Eurocomment by "Mercator", a pseudonym I was to resurrect in the 1980s. In it I sometimes criticised the Germans, who used Helmut Clissmann as a conduit for their displeasure. I used to pity poor Helmut, who found his task quite embarrassing.

But worse was to come. The new cemetery was opened in 1961. The German War Graves Commission had gathered together all they could find of relatives of the dead Germans of both wars to mark the occasion. In front of such an audience, the Ambassador, Dr. Felician Prill, made the most audaciously anti-Communist and anti-German Democratic Republic speech that I have ever heard. It was the wrong note to strike at such a solemn moment, and Karin and I walked out, publicly and openly. I went straight to the office and penned (I never typed) an excoriating leading article. I have yet to be invited to another function in the embassy.

Germany was never far from my mind. Dr. Kurt Ticher, a Dublin woollen merchant and, with his wife, a writer on and serious collector of Irish silver[47] since the 1930s, invited me to Germany for the Leipzig Fair and I accepted. I spent a week or so there, in the badly-scarred city trying to rise from its knees. I remember the smell from some of the roadside drains: it struck me as odd that this novel aroma should not have been dealt with before the Western world arrived to sample the German Democratic Republic's finest wares.

But I was growing accustomed to the people and sights that I met. I sensed a spirit of sacrifice and humility that stood in marked contrast to the arrogance and conspicuous affluence of the West Germans. In 1954, my grandmother-in-law, my *Kleine Oma*, took Karin and me to a new and luxurious café in Düsseldorf. She looked around at the fine décor, the napery, the delph and the silverware, sighed and said: *"Na ja, wir können's ja, wir haben's ja, das geld ist noch da".* (Ah well, we can do it, we have it, the money is there).

So I was well conditioned to receive an invitation to tour the country. As we sped through Weimar towards Berlin, I sang the words of Becher and Eisler's fine national anthem of the GDR, and thus drew the attention of our guide to myself. We were a mixed bag; an Englishman who had known Michael Viney in Hove, a Czech called Svoboda, which I discovered was the Czech equivalent of Murphy, and a dozen others from West and Eastern Europe. I should not have been surprised when I was asked to stay on after the tour and meet some more senior people from the Central Press Office for a talk in Berlin.

But first we had to see the Wall, built in 1961, two years before our trip. At the Brandenburg Gate, we were ushered into a room in the arch where a Volksarmée colonel told us why they had built the wall - first to quell the disastrous tide of people flowing West; and secondly to protect the value of the East German mark, which had been trading at a calamitous four to one against the Deutschmark.

The barrier was low in front of the gate and we were able to view the Westerners viewing us from a platform. After lunch, our Berlin guide left us for the afternoon, and when we met her for dinner I asked her how she had spent the afternoon. "Crying", she said. "Why?", I asked. "Because there we were, a few feet from the Wall. I could easily have jumped it and with you Western journalists watching, they would not have dared to shoot me". "But why do you want to go to the West?" "I want to see Selfridges", she sobbed.

At the initial meeting in an anonymous Berlin office building there were two or three of them and one of me. I now suppose they were Stasi using the Central Press Office as a cover. They wanted me to act as their eyes and ears in Ireland, to go to meetings abroad and report my findings to them. They were intensely curious about the West. They felt totally cut off by the Wall and they needed to know how the West saw them and how the West would react in given politico-military situations. They were especially interested in NATO Council meetings, which they felt I could cover in the normal course of my work.

I was flattered, intrigued and curious about the prospect of entering the world of John Le Carré. And I was most of the time fairly drunk. They would pay my expenses and a fee which would be commensurate with the value of my reports. I was also, I suppose, eager to help the socialist/communist underdogs in a world which reviled them.

Details were discussed. The method of entry - Check-point Charlie was not the only one; the method of payment, always in West German Deutschmarks since the DDR mark was not convertible; the concealment of cash in my shoes; the use of a code name, Paddy O'Brien, for me. I don't remember much more, and since my address book with their coded names and addresses and telephone numbers was later mislaid, I have no record of their names. A Dr. Neumann I do recall because some months later we took a long slow train through northern Germany to Stralsund in the snow. At the hotel there, I ordered a bear steak from the menu out of curiosity "We haven't seen a bear for ten years", said the waiter. I still don't know why we made this tedious journey. I did see the shipyards, but we stayed only one night, which ended with an early-morning call (3.30) and involved lugging my heavy Samsonite suitcase all the way to the station. Neumann said no taxi-driver would venture out so early and in the snow.

I felt like a strange mixture of honoured guest and paid agent. They invited Karin and me to a Jugendtreffe at Whitsuntide of 1964. The city was giving visas to people under 25 from the West, and Berlin was thronged. There were 24 bands in the crowded streets playing anything from jazz to Strauss. The pavement stalls on Unter den Linden and all around served sausages and vodka and there was no lower age limit, so we saw numbers of 14-year-olds tippling away. The climax was a gigantic fireworks display, the like of which I have never seen since.

Karin and I must have discussed what I was doing, but I have no recollection of our having done so. I know that she did agree to take a report from me to Brussels, where she was going to meet Seán MacBride at the Metropole Hotel. She had one half of a piece of costume jewellery and the messenger from Berlin carried the other half as proof of his authenticity. Two years later, Karin was in Berlin making a highly critical report for Amnesty International on the DDR's treatment of political prisoners and being interviewed by *Der Tagesspiegel* (8.5.66).

What, you might ask, was the nature of my reports to these people? In short, harmless. I took a few diplomats to lunch in Dublin to obtain their view of issues of the day in Europe. Of them, I remember only Bo somebody from the Swedish Embassy. I had, as I have shown, no direct contact with the West German mission. I could glean nuggets from *The Economist* and other serious periodicals, especially from the American Embassy, but they were all in the public domain.

I went to Berlin perhaps half-a-dozen times, flying Dublin-London-Hamburg-Berlin Tempelhof and staying in the Sofia, once in the still-intact remnant of the splendid old Adlon, and several times in the Gästehaus der Regierung, the Government Guest House. At the Sofia, my mentor taught me how to make and drink Nikolaschka. Take a brandy ballon. Add a tailor of brandy (less than a half measure). Place a slice of lemon across the top. Place half a teaspoon of sugar and a similar amount of ground coffee on the lemon. Scoff the lot, chewing sugar, coffee, lemon juice and brandy as the mixture goes down. I got Gus Weldon of the Pearl Bar to make them for George, Donald and me. Gus's problem was to put a price on a Nikolaschka. He settled for 3s. 6d.

I got a few frights. Coming back through Checkpoint Charlie with cash concealed in my shoes and undeclared, and being made to wait for hours in that cold shed. Being instructed at the last minute to depart through the Friedrichstrasse S-bahn exit, where the officials had no record of how I got in. Seeing a man I had met in Berlin striding down O'Connell Street in Dublin. He avoided me. He was attached to the DDR's London trade office and presumably had arrived in Ireland in the normal visa-free way.

I suppose you could say I was playing games, perhaps acting out some of my father's fantasies. I mastered, as he had, the art of leaving the office for the week-end without anybody's knowing where I had been. The whole episode lasted no more than eighteen months and was terminated by me on the pretence that I was being watched by the CIA. I heard no more and did not return to the East until 1993, when I found Wittenberg a sad neglected place to be, though it boasted an Irish Pub.

Since I drank alcoholically for 30 years, I could not say that my essay into espionage was more drunken than any other part of my life. I can only imagine that I would not have accepted the invitation if I had been sober.

CHAPTER 20

FAUGH A BALLAGH

In 1963, I had another German adventure. I was features editor when the Headquarters of the Royal Irish Fusiliers at Lisburn telephoned to ask if *The Irish Times* would be interested in sending a representative to Celle, near Hanover, where the Fusiliers were being presented with new colours by Field Marshal Lord Templer, CIGS. I said yes please, I would go myself.

It was an extraordinary time for me. My daughter Kristin was already in Germany with Lotte Brase (now Eimer), her nanny. The Brases lived at Lobmachtersen, near Salzgitter where the marvellous DART system of Dublin was made, so when the colours ceremony was being rehearsed, I was able to invite Lotte and Kristin to the barrack square in Celle.

The fine barracks was a pre-war construction taken from the German Army intact. The Royal Irish Fusiliers (later merged with the Inniskillings to form the Royal Irish Rifles) were a very mixed lot. In the ranks were lads from Sallynoggin, the Shankill and Jamaica. Among the officers were many Irishmen from North and South, Clongowes and Campbell. Colonel Linford commanded the regiment, and among the guests was Brigadier Morgan The O'Donovan MC, my namesake and the head of my clan. The O'Donovan lived at Hollybrook House, Skibbereen, Co. Cork. He had retired from the regiment in 1944, when he was 51.

It was a time to show off the regiment to the top brass. A regiment gets new colours only every 25 years, so a major event was being made of this one. In brilliant sunshine, and to the stirring music of the regimental pipe band, the troops performed the most complicated choreography. Quite gratuitously and most ungraciously, Colonel Linford told the troops before he dismissed them: "Let's do better next time chaps".

There was a regimental ball that night. I was too drunk to appreciate the lovely evening gowns and uniforms and retired early to bed. With whiskey at sixpence a glass, perhaps even an alcoholic could be excused from dancing. But I did see Belsen, the concentration camp that Denis Johnston wrote about so movingly in his autobiography [48]. And I did meet Blanaid Reddin, later of Bord Fáilte. A daughter of Dr. "Dempo" Reddin and relative of a distinguished family that included District Justice Kenneth Reddin, who wrote novels under the pen-name Kenneth Sarr, Blanaid was in charge of the NAAFI in Celle and clearly was a most popular member of the Fusiliers' family.

I wrote a long article about the regiment for the paper and sent it ahead of me with a Northern journalist, Trevor Hanna. Such was the state of technology then, though I could have typed it if I had been able to type. I was amazed to see the splash that Alan Montgomery gave it. Complete with four photographs, it looked like a recruiting poster for the British Army. The regiment was highly pleased, and so was I.

Germany had figured earlier in my journalistic life, when I was invited to tour the country with an international group of journalists covering the Eucharistic Congress of 1960. We began our itinerary in Munich, where Karin was looking after a coachload of members of the Irish-German Society. She and I were lodged in a tenement house (Munich was crammed with visitors) allotted to us. The lavatory was common, down two broad flights of stone steps, and the landlady addressed us as *die Herrschaften*, as in "What would your lordships like for breakfast in the morning?" Bavaria was still very Catholic. For all I know, it may yet be so.

My group and I saw Dinkelsbühl and Rothenburg on the Tauber, all those cherished medieval towns that are so lovingly conserved. When we got to Cologne, our guide told us he was taking us to the best restaurant in Germany. Halfway through a superb meal, he got cross. "Do you see that?", he asked us. "That", was two waiters, tables away from us having a chat. "That should never happen in a good restaurant", he pronounced.

Among us were two priest-journalists from India. More different people you could not imagine. Father Benny Aguiar was a Goan working in Bombay, tall, handsome, a man of the world. Father Joseph Thaikoodan was dark-skinned, from Kerala and always ate his dinner backwards - pudding first, starter afterward. Yet they were friends and said Mass together wherever they could find an obliging parish priest.

Emmett O'Connell, the Irish-American entrepreneur. Born in 1936 in the Bronx, New York, he has engaged in many enterprises including trading in gold and publishing in Dublin, and oil exploration around the world. He is called after Robert Emmet but his father was not a good speller. Now living in Co. Wexford, Emmett loomed large in my first book, "Dreamers of Dreams". To interview him, I flew to San Antonio, Texas.

CHAPTER 21

THE LAST ARNOTT

About this time I got to know John Arnott, a member of the family that bought *The Irish Times* in 1873. Sir John Arnott was a swarthy, good-looking, mischievous man who became London Editor of the paper. Hugh Oram[49] says of John that he "gave the impression of being an Empire Loyalist, very upper class, tapping out the 'London Letter'". Well, he had been to one of the good schools and he had the accent to prove it. But John was a good, kind, generous man who, perhaps like myself, did not like the changes that were occurring in our world. Oram says [49] that he and Donal Foley, his assistant in London, made "a bizarre match". And they did. Foley was a socialist of very great ability and a broad vision which he got the opportunity to enlarge when he became News Editor and hired the paper's talented group of women journalists. I have to say that I did not like Donal Foley in those later years. I felt that he was jealous of me and that we were in competition for the editorship. As we were both Catholics by upbringing, there was little chance of that, though it did happen when Conor Brady was appointed years later, in 1986. As my performance diminished and Foley's influence grew, he exploited my vulnerability and whenever I took the afternoon editorial conference, he subtly sought to belittle me. Maybe I'm wrong, but that's how I saw it.

John - this would have been in the early 1960s - hatched a plan to take over the paper (John still had 17,500 shares). He got Lord Glenavy's agreement to take over as Chairman of the board and he wanted me as Editor, himself presumably as Chief Executive. But the directors persuaded John to sell his shares to them. The shares would be divided equally among them and as they said they expected never to get a dividend, John for the good of the paper sold.

What happened next turned out quite differently from what John Arnott could have expected. On Friday 5 April 1974, *The Irish Times* announced on page one a major change of direction.

To set up *The Irish Times* as "a serious and independent newspaper", a trust was established by the five directors "who represent equally the whole of the ordinary stock". This it was stated, was being done because of their concern that through "the dispersal of stock holdings and other events, *The Irish Times* might become controlled by proprietors who might not maintain those standards".

Among the many worthy objectives then set out was one to make sure that the Editor and "every future editor" shall also be a director of the company.

To finance this scheme, the ordinary stockholders sold their stock to an unlimited holding company called The Irish Times Holdings for £1,625,000. The other stock (51/2% Preference and 61/2% Second Preference Stock) was also brought, for £380,000 at the full par value. The Investment Bank of Ireland provided the £2 million finance necessary to make possible the creation of The Irish Times Trust Ltd. under a board of governors who would also be the directors of the holding company and the governors of The Irish Times Foundation Limited, which was to have "exclusively charitable objects".

The governors were listed as:
> T.B. McDowell, chairman and managing director of The Irish Times Limited.
> Thekla Beere, chairman of the Commission on the Status of Women.
> William Blease, Northern Ireland Officer, Irish Congress of Trade Unions.
> John Healy, journalist.
> James Meenan, chairman of the Royal Dublin Society.
> Donal Nevin, assistant general secretary of the Irish Congress of Trade Unions.
> Peter O'Hara, group financial director of Brooks Watson and formerly director of administration Northern Ireland Housing Executive.
> James Walmsley, chairman of Eason and Son Ltd.
> Jacob Weingreen, Professor of Hebrew, Trinity College, Dublin.
> Richard Wood, chairman of J.A. Wood Ltd.

Major McDowell was to continue as chairman and managing director of

The Irish Times Limited and Mr. Douglas Gageby was to continue as Editor of *The Irish Times* and editorial director of the company. Ralph Walker, Philip Walker and George Hetherington retired from the board. Each of the five received £325,000 from the money provided by the Investment Bank of Ireland.

"The trust company", said the statement, "will nominate from among their own number the majority of directors of the board of The Irish Times Ltd."

It was a complex arrangement, and one that could be faulted for its complexity. But in the light of subsequent developments in the media industry in Ireland, it has to be said that we are fortunate to have a strong, independent newspaper that maintains the separation between business, politics and the media, and has the courage to speak out when others transgress. I like to think that John Arnott would have agreed.

The Arnotts had founded the Phoenix Park Racecourse in 1902 and John was always good to George Leitch and myself, giving us free entrance tickets and inviting us up to the Directors' bar. He married late and died young. I did not meet his wife Annie but I would like to wish her well.

When in 1961 Ireland (with England) was rejected by General de Gaulle as a member of the EEC, I had just completed a tour of the six founding countries. I wrote a series of twelve articles and was praised for them by the chairman, Ralph Walker. This was at the inauguration of a novel idea, an annual executives' lunch at the Shelbourne Hotel. The paper had just introduced colour to its pages, and Conor Cruise O'Brien had just married Máire MacEntee, his colleague in External Affairs. Cruise O'Brien's wife, Christine Foster, became the wife of George Hetherington, a director of *The Irish Times* and owner of Hely's the printers. In his speech after lunch, Hetherington suggested that we all had had enough of colour in our lives. As if in sympathy, the executive lunch died a death too.

It was Martin Sheridan, the CTT man whose departure from *The Irish Times* had led to my sudden elevation to the editorial department in 1957, that suggested my name to Michael Rice. Michael Rice was the head of a major London public relations consultancy. He already knew Donal Carroll of the eponymous cigarette manufactory, so when Carroll decided to launch the Peter Stuyvesant brand on the Irish market in 1960, he brought in Michael's firm. Michael felt that he needed an Irish connection and Martin Sheridan provided it in me.

Donal Carroll, Michael Rice and myself are the same age, give or take three months, and we formed a good team. Anton Rupert of Rothman's cigarettes had a shareholding in Carrolls, who were to make Stuyvesant in Dundalk. The cigarette had a modestly successful launch, one result of which was that for 19 years afterward I was to receive a carton of 200 cigarettes every fortnight. I stopped smoking in 1972, but the cigarettes rolled in and were useful for spot-prizes and hospital comforts at Christmas.

The Rice friendship grew as Michael and I tried to get big corporate clients in this country. Michael Rice (Ireland) Ltd. was formed with me as the Irish director and a fine office in Leeson Street. This house, No. 72, had an apartment upstairs which on occasions I used as a pied-à-terre for amatory adventures. George Hayes was our valet and general factotum, a welcome face at the bedroom door as he asked: "How many for breakfast this morning, sir?".

The office was managed by John Fraser and Bill Hodnett, a man of great charm and fun. Unfortunately, he and Michael did not generate the right kind of chemistry. John Fraser, a nice Englishman, did not suit and was not comfortable with the Irish business landscape. You must remember too that P.R. was in its infancy, so that while I secured time for a long presentation to Jack Lynch as Minister for Industry and Commerce, the mention of £20,000 as our fee for enhancing the image of Ireland Inc. was beyond Lynch's ken. When Fraser left, Bill Hodnett tried to hold the place together with Maeve O'Connor-Cox, our splendid secretary.

I got to know Donal Carroll well. He surprised me one night by making an impassioned speech in which he outlined his vision of Ireland. This was a private session and gave me great heart. He was the man who more than any other rationalised the Irish banking system, merging the National Bank and the Hibernian Bank into the Bank of Ireland and also in 1960, founding Foster Finance, later Bank of Ireland Finance.

When he asked me in 1969 to join the Bank of Ireland, he meant well. But I did not realise that he was leaving the governorship and in effect abandoning me to the wily wolves. He went to London as deputy chairman of Lloyds International expecting to move into the chair and being mistaken. The job I took was not the job as painted by Pat Elliott, another Carroll appointment. "At our level, Donal, we take the afternoon off when we want to", said Pat when we were lunching at the Intercontinental. Elliott, a jazz fiend, did not belong to the culture of the bank and he left after some years to take a bank-funded research fellowship at Trinity College.

At the pyramid of Gizeh in 1962. I'm eighth from left at back.

Raffe Roberts was another cultural error. While I was there, he was a lonely man who in my early days made me sit across from him talking for hours after the office at Hume House was closed. He did supervise the reworking of the bank's logo and signage, an incredibly expensive job done by an American called Doug Kelly. But Raffe too was moved on in time. He was given the top floor of No. 5 Merrion Square (a Foster Finance office). He was told to take it easy and write a report on youth sailtraining for the board. His salary was undiminished and the Volvo 240 was his to keep. Raffe died in a few short years, the report as far as I know undelivered. He left no family.

In the meanwhile Michael Rice and Company was not thriving in this country, partly because of my drinking but mainly because Irish industry was not ready for the spin doctor. In 1965, I was asked by Major T.B. McDowell, chief executive of *The Irish Times*, to create and edit a two-page business section to run daily. One condition was to relinquish my directorship of Michael's company. I was compensated for my small director's fee, but of course I also lost the use of the company Cortina and the occasional consorting that went on upstairs at No. 72.

Michael remained a friend for many years as he established himself as an Arabist, an archaeologist, a highly effective public relations presence in the Middle

East, and finally the designer of a series of eight most beautiful and costly Islamic museums at Qatar, Oman and sites in Saudia Arabia. He is also the author of several books. Through him I met some M.P.s, had tea on the terrace of the House with William Rees-Mogg, then Editor of *The Times*, and went on a memorable facility visit to Egypt, where I had a suite in Shepheard's Hotel and a servant who scrubbed me in the bath, dried me off and washed my underclothes. Need I add that he was male? The belly dancer was good too, and although Gamal Abdel Nasser had just banned the Twist as occidental and degenerate, the owners of the riverboat restaurant let us dance the night away to the fashion of the moment.

Richard Hoggart (left) with me and Michael Rice at the second European Museum of the Year Awards ceremony, held in London in 1978. Richard Hoggart, formerly Assistant Director-General of UNESCO, was then Warden of Goldsmiths' College in the University of London.
Picture by Carole Easton.

CHAPTER 22

DUM DUM

Hugh O'Neill, now Lord Rathcavan and for many years chairman of the Northern Ireland Tourist Board, joined me in the business section of *The Irish Times*. We had a major launch at the Savoy in London with all sorts of City people and M.P.s there. As our guest of honour, I invited Donogh O'Malley, then Parliamentary Secretary to the Minister for Finance. Donogh had just given up alcohol and said he would come if I made sure he had a jug of milk beside him at all times. In my book, "God's Architect", [50] I say of him:

> O' Malley, while not a maverick, was *sui generis*, a rumbustious Limerick man with a quirky sense of humour and a joie de vivre that distinguished him from the grey men in grey suits that fill the ranks of most Governments. He had a special relationship with Éamon de Valera and delighted in telling the author the story of his summons to the President's house for a scolding:
>
> "They tell me, O'Malley, that you broke a plate-glass window in Limerick last night".
>
> "I did, Chief".
>
> "And what's more, O' Malley, they tell me you were drunk at the time".
>
> "Yerra Jasus, Chief, do you think I'd have done it if I wasn't? And what's more, Chief, they tell *me* that *you* slept with Mary MacSwiney".
>
> "Well you can tell them that's a lie", roared de Valera, thumping the study table.

As Minister for Education from 1966 until his awful death from a massive heart attack in 1968, Donogh introduced free secondary schooling which, says Louis McRedmond's "Modern Irish Lives" [51] "was arguably the most important development of the century in Irish education and made possible successful careers at home and abroad for thousands of young people over the following decades".

Donogh O'Malley I counted as a friend. We shared many a bar counter in Dublin and Limerick and made his policeman driver endure a few long nights' waiting while we pursued whatever it was we were pursuing.

Donogh O'Malley
- Lensmen

The friendship went sour over Terry Keane, with whom he was besotted and obsessed. His jealousy, for which there was no ground, went as far as telephoning the Pearl Bar in Fleet Street to tell Terry that his informants had just told him that I was having an afternoon drink with her. The end for me came at a reception in the Building Centre where he looked the other way when I greeted him. He died soon afterwards and that incident made his funeral in Limerick more poignant for me.

Before we both weep, let me tell you a second tale of Dum Dum. O'Malley was guest of honour at the launching of Mary Hanley's creation, the Kiltartan Society, which was founded to revere the poet William Butler Yeats. Mary was, as we used to say, vaccinated with a gramophone needle. As her introductory speech went on and on, Donogh wondered how he was going to wake the sleeping audience. When she finally stopped, Donogh turned to her and intoned: "Hail Mary, full of Yeats".

I seem to be galloping over the Sixties when I should be lingering in a rose garden. Joan Miller, who married Séamus of the Met Service because, she told me, Séamus needed her more than I did, was my companion in the garden of the lovely mountain hotel that Cyril Count McCormack owned on the Dublin-Wicklow border. Old Conna it was called. It is now Aravon school in the good care of Terence O'Malley. We had had lunch a couple of tables away from Kim Novak, who was filming Somerset Maugham's "The Razor's Edge" with Laurence Harvey. And under a cloudless sky we walked alone in that bower of roses. It was a memory to cherish.

The Sixties were special not only for me. Ken Whitaker with his grey book "Economic Development", unlocked the door into a new prosperity. We knew the Forties and Fifties had been dark places. We had seen the population haemorrhaging into England and America, the cultural desert they left behind. We had been buffeted by the Battle of Baltinglass and the Mother and Child scheme. We were down and out, spiritually and economically.

Then Martin Sidney the tailor from South King Street took a hand. He clothed a generation of young Government Ministers in mohair suits and suddenly Charlie Haughey, Brian Lenihan and Donogh O'Malley were given their heads by Seán Lemass. These are the ones I knew best. There was, until 8 October 1964, one more. I developed a kind of father-son relationship with Paddy Smith the Minister for Agriculture, whom I met through Dan Mullane of the Irish Flour Millers' Association. Dan was a wild man and he brought me to the George in Limerick to meet Paddy Smith, the farmer from Cavan who joined the Volunteers in 1918 and two years later was a battalion commander. He was sentenced to death for high treason in 1921, was saved by the Truce and after the Treaty fought in the Civil War. For over 50 years, from 1923 to 1977, he was a Dáil deputy but he never got on with Lemass and in 1964 resigned his portfolio in protest against "the tyranny" of the trades unions. This was a reference to efforts being made to settle a long building strike, a dispute that held no benefit for farmers. Another version, Hickey and Doherty's [52], has Smith resigning over milk subsidies. At any rate, Lemass within hours appointed his son-in-law Charlie Haughey, depriving Smith of the chance of holding a press conference. The urban-rural chasm widened.

Paddy Smith and I, twenty-seven years between us, became friends at once. We went from the George to Co. Clare, where the Minister opened a pig-finishing station. After a meal, we discarded his State car on the grounds, he said, that my Cortina was more comfortable. A mammoth pub-crawl ensued. It ended in a shebeen at the arse-end of Clare where the woman of the house served us mulled stout. That is to say, she put pints of Guinness on the hearth in front of us and took reddened pokers out of the turf fire, placed them in the pints and thus gave us hot stout. I think the flavour was different, but by this time we were reddened ourselves. It was a great day, and our friendship developed past a dinner in the Beaufield Mews in Stillorgan which was given by the National Farmers' Association or the *Farmers' Journal*, I forget which, as a kind of wake for the resigned Minister. Haughey, who was to get into serious trouble with the NFA led by Rickard Deasy, was not there. I can still hear Paddy Smith's voice saying: "Listen here to me now, Donovan".

With the young tigers I was very friendly, but not in the same way. I became a member of the Press Gallery and got parking at Leinster House for "my" car. I got a call from O'Malley one day to say that if I got down to the House that afternoon I might hear something that would give me a story. Right enough, the Minister for Finance, Dr. Jim Ryan, rose to speak on something innocuous and slipped in a mumbled announcement that he was increasing the duty on cigarettes by a penny from midnight. I got on the telephone. Nobody else had heard.

I could walk into Haughey's office in Leinster House to discuss something I wanted to write about in the next day's paper and I could dine and wine there or in the Shelbourne or Hibernian any night. These were the glory days, power without responsibility.

The tradition that the Editor wrote the leading article was a fiction seen through by a good P.R. man. Thus, for example, Dr. Jerry Dempsey of Aer Lingus could discover who precisely had written a given leader and ask him (there were no hers then) to lunch. There he could argue the airline's case with me and put me right where necessary. Jerry, who later became a member of the Bank of Ireland's court of directors, was damn all use to me in my days in the bank, when I wanted to lever up the clout I did not possess. Nor was Donal Carroll disposed to give me support, even when I went to Lloyd's International in London to see him.

Both Jerry Dempsey and Donal Carroll were more open to a journalist than to a bank manager, and Jerry, for example, would answer a question such as why did you make Desmond Fennell your manager for Germany and why did he leave? "It was", he said, "an experiment that failed". Desmond, who is a distinguished journalist and writer, went on to become Editor of *Herder Korrespondenz*, an intellectual Catholic magazine of European importance. Jerry was always accompanied at these lunches by his trusted lieutenant, Major Éamonn Rooney.

Brenda Fricker, then or thereabouts.

Dr. C.S. Andrews didn't need a P.R. man to get to me. Todd knew me from a child, as the man said, and we ate in Jammet's restaurant fairly often, sometimes with Karin. He would discuss CIE's affairs and make frank statements such as: "How can I negotiate with John Conroy (general president of the ITGWU) when I have a salary of £4,500 and he's on £1,500? It doesn't make sense".

Some time in 1965, I noticed that George Leitch had a new and lovely secretary. Brenda Fricker was working out the time that does not appear in the profiles. She says I was a terrible bastard, coming up to her eyrie every morning to demand crossly to see what markings there were for photographers that day. Until I noticed her pale golden beauty. We fell hard and spent hours in the Pearl Bar, on the beach in Killiney, where she gave me a stone that I treasured and then lost, and in her flat. The flat was shared by Ann Kavanagh whom we called the Reverend Mother.

I could truthfully tell her worried father, that lovely man Des Fricker, known professionally as Fred Desmond the broadcaster, that I had not slept with his 21 year old daughter. I was 38. Our "affair" lasted for a few years and is a very special part of my life. As Brenda rose to fame, getting an Oscar for her part in Jim Sheridan's "My Left Foot", she married Barry Davis, the well-known English television producer. His early death left her shattered but she has built up a solid reputation on both the small and the big screen.

CHAPTER 23

AMERICA AT LAST

"I packed my bag for Boston, and into it I put . . ." The old children's party game came to my mind when I set out for America for the first of many trips. I was gathering material for an advertising supplement on American-Irish trade, and I was concentrating on the East coast. I stayed first at the Parker House in Boston, a fabled hotel that featured with its owner, Jack Dunfey, in my first book[53].

This hotel was acquired in 1976, along with 13 others in the chain, by Aer Lingus. It has a long tradition, beginning in 1855 with a French chef reported around the town to be earning $5,000 when a good chef could be had for $8 a week. William Makepeace Thackeray contended that a plump Wellfleet oyster at the Parker House made him feel as though he were swallowing a baby. This remark was taken to be a compliment.

Jack Dunfey

Other guests enhanced the reputation of the Parker House. Henry Irving, Ellen Terry and Sarah Bernhardt were welcome, but John Wilkes Booth, who stayed there only eight days before he shot President Lincoln, did not make Harvey Parker feel especially proud. The Saturday Club met there and in 1857 published the first issue of the *Atlantic Monthly*. Among the early members of the club were Emerson, Oliver Wendell

Holmes, Nathanial Hawthorne and Longfellow, who sat with silver hair and beard at the foot of the table.

Ten years later, Charles Dickens wrote to his daughter: "The cost of living is enormous, but happily we can afford it. I dine today with Longfellow, Emerson, Holmes and Agassiz".

In New York, I knew nobody but Maeve Fitzgibbon. Still happily with us, Maeve represented SFADCO and was the unwitting cause of a restaurant's being born. She took me to lunch in Charlie Brown's in the giant PanAm Building The five Jewish gentlemen who owned Charlie Brown's serendipitously saw the supplement, thought that an Irish restaurant would enhance their business, and so Charley O's was built. Where exactly I forget, somewhere off Fifth Avenue and on about 50th Street. That was in 1965.

The greatest discovery I made in New York was Gordon Clark, who was Bord Fáilte's man in town. Gordon was one of the most knowledgeable men I have known. (He died of cancer many years ago.) Through him I met Walter J.P. Curley, later to be appointed U.S. Ambassador to Ireland. Curley was an associate of John Hay Whitney the financier. Both were very comfortably off as I found when Gordon left us in Lamb's, a discreet sort of club, and we went to Curley's apartment to share a can of beans. I can still see his children reporting one by one on how their day had gone and bidding us a formal goodnight. Only the rich have the confidence to offer a guest baked beans.

I was struck by the openness of American businessmen. At Merrill Lynch Pierce Fenner and Bean (known then as the Thundering Herd), I called unannounced to request an interview with the chairman of this financial giant. Not only did his secretary take my blue Crombie to sew on a dodgy button for me; I was taken to the boardroom and joined the directors for coffee.

I got a scoop in New York too. At home one of the burning issues of the day was the compulsory stopover at Shannon for planes bringing passengers from the United States to Dublin. It was resolved only recently, but then Aer Lingus and the Government were so touchy about an indefensible regulation that they were not prepared to talk to the likes of me. By telephoning Aer Lingus' New York lawyer, I got the whole story with no "given to understand or led to believe" cloaking the issue.

In Washington too, I could talk to anybody about anything. I got two stories to telephone to Hugh O'Neill. One I can't recall; the other was about the Irish Sugar Company. General Costello had lobbied hard and got a 10,000 ton quota for Irish sugar on the American market. When the time came to deliver, we didn't have anything like 10,000 tons to sell, but at home, nobody was prepared to tell me what or why. A call to the Department of Commerce led to an appointment with the right man - and an embarrassment for the General.

Washington, in spite of the kindness of the Ambassador, William Fay, and his staff, I thought a dreary provincial town, but over the years I have come to admire its beauty. Noel Dorr was a third secretary then and recklessly lent me his Volkswagen Beetle to drive through the snow to Maryland. He also lent me a Günther Grass novel (not "The Tin Drum") which I don't think I ever returned.

Syrian Arab Airlines flew Karin and me to Damascus. We had to go through Heathrow and when we arrived in Syria found that our luggage was missing. Delay, mystery, blame ensued, but in the heel of the hunt it was Aer Lingus who had lost the bags at London. Our Syrian hosts - the Government airline - very kindly brought us to the bazaar in Damascus and bought us the basics, including a lovely dark red silk dressing gown embroidered with gold thread. This was for me and it lasted for years as a fancy-dress costume, combined with a fez that I had bought in Cairo.

Damascus was a wonder. Nobody seemed to go to bed in the world's oldest inhabited city. Constant din, not only from the muezzin who calls the faithful to prayer but from the street Arabs and the stall-holders. We stayed by choice in a purely Muslim hotel, soaking up the sights, sounds and smells.

We drove to Palmyra via Homs, a journey of 250 miles on which I simply had to take a bottle of Powers Gold Label. The Roman ruins were awe-inspiring, but I overdid the tourist bit by climbing to the top of a wall, walking along it and suddenly getting an attack of vertigo. I was stuck, unable to move for many minutes. Blame it on the drink.

Along an ancient street, our guide found a Roman coin outside a 2,000 year old shop. You can believe that it had lain there all that time waiting for us, or you can imagine that it was manufactured the day before by the little man in

Fumbally Lane who turns out the jokes you hear over the bar.

What was impressive was the strong feeling that Palmyra, like Damascus, was once a major mercantile centre, sending to Rome silks, spices and preserved fruits. Imperial buildings, public works and circuses were added by the Romans to the existing layer of Greek culture.

The town, now called Tadmur, had changed little since Caesar's time. Except that at 10.30 at night its electricity was turned off until nine the next morning. For us, the town generator was switched on at 7.30 a.m. so that I could use my electric razor. Where would you get service like that?

Back to Damascus to take a taxi to Amman. At the Jordan frontier, there was a hitch. We had to put our passports on a table in the customs post and we saw that among about 20 passports, three were Irish. When they were stamped and returned to the table, there were two Irish passports, ours. I asked the taxi-driver where the third one had gone:

"Oh, that belonged to a Dublin Jewish lady who was trying to see her daughter in Jerusalem. She was sent home".

"But how did she escape notice at Damascus?".
"Well, the Jordanians, you see, are better at catching Jews".

This was all happening in 1964, three years before the Arab-Israeli war of 1967. So after Amman, which I do not remember, we arrived by DC3 in Arab East Jerusalem where they showed us the olive trees that are older than Christ. Or so they said. The Intercontinental there was a relief from Damascus: the public lavatories in Jerusalem were totally disgusting. And the plane that brought us back had a hole in the roof of the toilet. It didn't matter because the DC3 was not pressurised, but it did not add to my feeling of security.

Back in Damascus again, I asked for an interview with the Minister of the Economy. There we sat, Karin in the room but not at his desk, worlds apart as we sized each other up. What to say?
"Minister, what is the level of unemployment in Syria?"
"What is the level in Ireland?"
"About 8 per cent".
"Ah yes, it would be about the same in Syria".

The truth, I discovered, was nearer to 80 percent. I never reported this interview, and Syrian Arab Airlines found it hard to push me to write anything about this wonderful week. I did a highly inaccurate piece, mainly about Palmyra, and invited the justified wrath of a reader in the letters column. Alcohol was a serious problem by now, though I would not face it.

A couple of years later, I met someone fairly senior in the Japanese Embassy. He sounded me out about writing a monthly report for him on the news behind the news. I did it for a year or so, giving him bits of gossip or additional information about stories that had appeared. A lot of the legwork was done by that decent *Irish Times* librarian Tony Lennon, and I got the princely sum of £30 a month. I could never fathom why the figure was always written in pencil on the receipt. Inscrutable, I suppose.

That was 1966, the year that Jack Lynch became Taoiseach. I was friendly with Jack and his lovely wife Máirín throughout the Sixties and early Seventies. But I worked hard to support Charlie Haughey in his heave against Lynch in 1979, the year I was Fianna Fáil Director of Elections for Wicklow in the European and local government elections. The dismal results of those elections and some by-elections, plus a growing feeling that Lynch was not altogether the innocent victim of Haughey and Blaney in the Arms affair of 1970 left me with high expectations that Haughey would straighten out the economy which was in a mess after Martin O'Donoghue's reckless election promises of 1977. And that Haughey would take a much stronger Republican line on the North. I was naïve to think that the aspirations expressed by a man hungry for power would be translated into realities once the gates of Government Buildings were opened to him.

I could put another spin on that statement by recalling Haughey's face-to-face remark when I asked him what it was like to be Taoiseach: "The job doesn't carry the power that I thought it did", he answered.

CHAPTER 24

JENNY

Now comes the important part of my personal life. Towards the end of May 1968, Douglas Gageby put his head around the door of the Features Department. "What in the name of God is wrong with you?", he asked. Out of nowhere came my reply: "I'm an alcoholic". "Okay", said Douglas, "go and do something about it".

My performance must have sunk to a new depth in an office so tolerant of drinking. I know that I had become a procrastinator, unable to deal with high-quality material being offered by people such as Mark Bence-Jones, unable to accept the talents displayed by people like Bruce Arnold for whom I conceived an irrational dislike, since rectified.

So like my good friend Paddy Delany the architect, I did something. I went to Paddy's doctor in Blackrock. "Nothing to worry about", said the good Dr. Arthur Brookes. "You've had your last drink. No need to go to hospital. Just come to me at nine every morning. I'll give you an injection of Vitamin B12 in your backside and you can go on to work. After three weeks or so you'll be over the withdrawals. Just don't drink again". The date was 31st May 1968 and I believed him.

Kristin and I had moved from Oaklands Drive to De Vesci Court, where we rented a new apartment. Dublin was slow to embrace the notion of apartment life and this block in Monkstown by John du Moulin was one of the pioneering developments. Leaving a load of furniture and equipment to be sold, we took what I thought were the best pieces and arranged them in what I thought was good taste. Kristin was twelve and while I was still drinking she felt lonely and isolated. People were very kind to us though, and we had a good social life with my peers, though not with hers. She was my escort at a lot of dinners, but she was pretty miserable at Park House School.

My only encounter with the bailiff was at Monkstown. I had failed to pay my rates and had answered no demand notes. The sheriff's men were due to take away my furniture when I telephoned Michael Hayes, the City Sheriff himself. Michael, a solicitor, was an old college friend, a son indeed of Michael Hayes who held the chair of Modern Irish at UCD and had been one of the speakers at my inaugural address. Michael called off the dogs and let me down gently. I don't know how he did it, but he saved the day for me.

Somewhere, somehow, some time, I met Jenny McGrath. We were introduced by Harriet Cooke, with whom I had a liaison for quite a while. She was a New Yorker separated from Barry Cooke the artist. A journalist, she wrote the text of a large supplement that the *The Irish Times* produced for the Stillorgan Shopping Centre, the country's first. That was in 1966. A year or so later, after Karin's death, I met Jenny. I had heard her name at parties all over the town and had decided that I liked what I heard.

Jenny was a gentle and beautiful woman of 30, divorced and living with her parents and her five-year-old son Julian. She worked with John O'Donovan, the irascible journalist whom I had first met in the *Evening Press*. Life had not been good to Jenny and she was finding social life in Dublin quite unforgiving for the divorcee. Not unusual then; not much better now.

Our first meeting, I think, was at a party given by the artist Patrick Pye. She may say otherwise: I was still drinking. When I went to Dr. Brookes, who said my liver was enlarged though not irreparable, I was able to present my real self to Jenny, and we talked for hours on end in front of the fire at Monkstown. I told her all about my alcoholism, now, I assured her, a thing of the past. And one evening, to please me, she brought a tasty coq au vin for dinner with Michael and Ethna Viney.

A long time afterwards, she told me that when Karin died, Jenny's Texan mother Mary Catherine read the appreciation in *The Irish Times* and said to her: "There you are. There's a good man available for you. Go get". That was not Jenny's style at all, and it was I who made the running: I wanted to get engaged and married as soon as was decent.

Kristin and I went to England that summer of 1968. We saw the sights of London. I met Barbara Smith for the last time and we went down to Harting in Hampshire to see Jenny and Julian. Jenny was enceinte and noticeably so, but it came as no surprise to me. I had known for some time that she was expecting a child by a man whom I later got to know in another context.

It was in my mind to adopt the child, but Jenny was not ready for such a drastic move. She thought, and I'm sure she was right, that to add another infant to the family we already had in Kristin and Julian would cause an upheaval that we could not cope with. Jenny had her daughter in the local cottage hospital and named her Marina. She had arranged for her to be adopted six months before.

Much heart and soul searching went on for years for Jenny especially around the time of Marina's birthday, 11 August. Eventually, she felt the time had come to tell the children, who now included Síofra. Jenny was quite fearful about telling them, but she need not have worried. They were all pleased to hear that they had a sister, and Síofra especially was not only excited but quite determined that Jenny should make whatever moves were necessary to find her.

Jenny felt the time was right - this was in 1994 when Síofra was 23 - and she contacted Catherine House, London. And the miracle happened. Within a week or so of one another Jenny and Marina wrote to Catherine House asking for help.

In no time, they were in touch by post, and by November 1994, I drove to Dublin Airport, collected "my" new daughter, deposited her with Jenny and went to bed in my sister Sheila's house. Marina had come home. She is now (1997) 29 years old and working with disadvantaged children in Bogotá, Colombia. She is one of the world's wonderful people, strikingly beautiful, compassionate, humorous and in the literal sense skilful.

In the months before we married, Jenny told me all about her life with Derk Kinnane, a fellow journalist and Gate Theatre actor from New York. I think Derk, with whom I still correspond, thought he was Orson Welles reincarnated. MacLiammóir called Derk his "little Dutch tulip" because Derk's father was a Roelofsma from Friesland. The trouble was that he too was alcoholic, so Jenny was jumping from an American frying pan into an Irish fire.

When he heard of my engagement, Micheál MacLiammóir wrote on 15 October 1968:

My Dear Donal,

You really are superb. I am quite crazy about you, which is a great compliment to you as we have known each other for such a comparatively short time. I am thrilled to hear that you are re-marrying: it proves the old theory that a burnt child loves the fire. But which Tuesday, you wonderful love-crazed creature? I would love to, but it can't be today . . . .

In the meanwhile, affectionate greetings to you, and my rather thoughtful blessings on you both.

Yours ever

Micheál

My father's feelings about my new status were different. When I went to see him at 114 Rathgar Road, he said first:

"I suppose she's a Protestant?"

"Yes".

"I suppose she's divorced?"

"Yes".

"Now listen. Gerard is married to a Dutch-Canadian Lutheran. Sheila is married to a Belfast Protestant. Aedine is married to a Hungarian living in Holland. You were married to a German atheist. Why couldn't one of you, just one, marry the girl next door?".

He was not very serious about it. In fact, I think he knew all about Jenny already, and he was very deliberately distorting Basil Hanna's background. Basil's Belfast Protestant father had become a Catholic in order to marry, and Basil, Sheila's husband, now dead, was born in Dublin. Jim and Ernest Hanna, Assistant Secretary to the Department of Finance, had become good friends through Sheila's marriage. And in the fullness of whatever time was left to him, Jim and Jenny got on very well. My mother too seemed pleased, and on the McGraths' getting-to-know-you visit to Rathgar, Jenny's only sibling Norman came along and there was hilarity all round. My parents must have been delighted to see me sober after twenty years.

Douglas and Dorothy Gageby gave a dinner party for our engagement. Bruce and Millie Williamson were the other guests and it was a happy gathering at which little or no alcohol was consumed.

Jenny's father was Raymond McGrath, the Principal Architect of the Board of Works and an R.H.A. of some distinction. He had been released from his normal duties to design the Kennedy Memorial Concert Hall and was within a few weeks of formal retirement. But people like Raymond do not retire. He was to go on working on the Concert Hall until five years later, when the project was finally axed in favour of the more modest building that now serves as the National Concert Hall.

Obviously I have a talent for selecting interesting fathers-in law. Raymond was a colonial, born in Gladesville on the Parramatta River near Sydney, Australia. He was of mixed stock, Irish and English, but he never in his heart felt anything but Australian. He maintained his nationality though because of his distinguished work on the acquisition and decoration of Irish embassies abroad, he carried an Irish diplomatic passport. These buildings benefited from Donegal Carpets and Waterford Glass chandeliers designed by Raymond, who had retained the right to private practice as an industrial designer and had been instrumental in the post-war revival of those two craft industries.

In the course of researching my book, "God's Architect" [54], I found a copy letter from me to Raymond thanking him for a very pleasant dinner at Somerton Lodge in 1964. It is a measure of my sickness that I have no recollection of having met this engaging, simple and artistic man until I began to have designs on his daughter. But clearly he was writing feature articles for me and we were relating well four years earlier.

After a brilliant and satisfying apprenticeship at Sydney University, Raymond became the first research student in architecture at Cambridge and was acclaimed internationally as the designer of Finella, a totally refurbished 1850 house on the Backs near his beloved Clare College.

The Thirties were Raymond's great years. He designed houses, radios and aircraft interiors, and he headed the team that decorated the new Broadcasting House. He became one of a small band of Modern Movement architects in England. And he wrote two seminal books - "Twentieth Century Houses" (1934, written in Basic English) and "Glass in Architecture and Decoration" (1937).

A great social life, influential friends, job satisfaction in abundance, and a happy marriage with two children were all his. In 1938, domestic bliss was marred by Mary Catherine's severe manic depression, a disorder which was to dog her life for 40 years.

The war brought further troubles. There was no work for architects and Raymond, having been commissioned by the War Artists' Advisory Committee to paint sixteen illustrations of the aircraft factories of Britain, settled for a job as senior architect with the Board of Works in Dublin. There he relieved the tedium of life in neutral Ireland by painting, eventually in the year of his death in 1977 becoming President of the Royal Hibernian Academy.

Neither the Church of Ireland to which Jenny nominally belonged, nor the Roman Catholic Church in which I had been baptised, wanted to marry a divorcee and a widower, so we settled for the registry office (then in Kildare Street). Mr Raymond Downey officiated.

It was a splendid wedding, forty guests in the Russell Hotel including both sets of parents, my father now in a wheelchair. Jenny and I had worked hard at the guest list. Clodagh Budd Maughan (now Studdert) was her matron of honour and my brother Gerry once again my best man. Jock Harbison made a thoughtful speech. I don't think Raymond spoke, but I, drinking non-alcoholic wines carefully chosen by Raymond, spoke and well too.

If Jenny was nervous, she did not show it. She looked, as the cliché goes, radiant, and it was a happy event, graced by Sir Ove Arup the celebrated engineer

Outside the Russell on our wedding day, 23 November 1968.
Left: Louise O Donovan, Jenny, Donal, Kristin and Gerry. Top left is Julian.

and his wife Li. The photographs are neither numerous nor of great quality, but they serve for us as warm reminders of a day that finished in Ennis, Co. Clare, where Vincent and Orla Tobin greeted our Mini as though it were a limousine drawing up to the front door of the Old Ground Hotel. We went on to tour Kerry next day and had a riotous honeymoon spoiled only by some food-poisoning. It was the last week in November, 1968, and Kerry could have been the South of France. The love that was growing deepened and soon we had a second honeymoon.

Leslie Knight was an associate of Michael Rice. He had particular charge of the Middle East. He asked me to do a consultancy report on the *Daily Star*, the English-language daily newspaper published in Beirut. I agreed on condition that, instead of a business-class flight and a first-class hotel, the Saint George, I could travel and live second-class (the Commodore) and bring my wife. Agreed.

Beirut was a revelation. I had expected the banking centre of the Middle East to look like Frankfurt. It had splendid hotels - the Phoenicia was the newest. Its corniche looked like the Côte d'Azur. But Islam and the Arab culture prevailed over the Maronites, and the Palestinians had penetrated the corridors of power.

We went in January, a cold January by their standards. The Editor of the

Eating out in Beirut, February 1969. From left: Francis Karam, Jenny, Mimi Karam and myself.

Daily Star was Francis Karam, a Palestinian. From 8 a.m. to 2 p.m., Francis was a bank clerk, then he changed hats and became a journalist until 10 p.m. I met them all but I can remember only Peggy Johnston, who wrote a daily column, and George Batten, Francis' right hand man. At dinner with these two men separately, and at other functions, the message was driven home: "If it takes us 2,000 years, we'll drive the Israelis into the sea". This was in 1969, two years after the '67 War but long before the Lebanon itself blew up.

I worked the same hours as Francis, talking to the staff individually, either on the job or at lunch at the Saint George. I asked endless questions, observed every action, made copious notes and presented my report, which Jenny typed for me. The management thanked me and paid me. I do not to this day know whether they accepted any or all of my recommendations but I do know that the building was bloody cold. The Lebanon knows how to keep the heat out and lays marble floors on its more important buildings. But when a cold snap comes, the country can't cope. It's like snow in Washington. Francis had to wait about ten days to get a three-bar electric heater from the administration: in the meanwhile we shivered.

I very much wanted Jenny to see Damascus, so we hired a taxi and set out. At the frontier we were stopped and our passports taken. A grim-faced official brought the documents back to us. "She can go: not you". The reason? "No journalists allowed". Such a change in five years! The 1967 war brought things to this pass. We went home to the Commodore. Jenny was finding plenty to do and see in Beirut anyway, and we had an exciting trip to the Beqa'a Valley to see the Roman remains at Baalbek.

Ireland's honorary consul-general in the Lebanon was Sir Desmond Cochrane of Woodbrook, that lovely house on the Dublin side of Bray. Sir Desmond was married to the Lebanese princess Yvonne Sursock, whose wealthy family had endowed a museum in Beirut.

I had written to him from Dublin and received a warm welcome to lunch. At drinks beforehand, Sir Desmond said:

"I'm surprised to have a visit from a second Irish journalist in ten days. The other fellow came from Teheran looking for Irish whiskey and Carroll's cigarettes for a St. Patrick's Day party. I couldn't help".

We were agog to know who this man was.

"Oh, his name was Kinnane. Yes, Derk Kinnane".

This was Jenny's first husband, the last man on earth that she wanted to see, in Beirut or anywhere. Derk was working on a paper in Teheran and had two American women colleagues whom I met later in the same year when I was riding a camel on the beach at Bombay. The world shrinks.

Between Sir Desmond's revelation and Lady Cochrane's insistence on speaking French to her other luncheon guests, I could not say that we enjoyed that meal. As we wandered around the streets afterwards we half expected to meet Derk around every corner.

Jenny and I at Somerton Lodge, 1969. Kristin in the background.

CHAPTER 25

A NEW LIFE

There were thorns on our roses. Think of our children, our bespoke family. Kristin suddenly ousted from her place as my escort and dinner companion. Julian, light of Mary Catherine's eye, reduced from three acres of freedom at Somerton Lodge to a small apartment in which he, at five, had to share a bunk bed with Kristin aged twelve. Kristin had two years of sullen misery, not eased by being removed from Park House School to Loreto Convent in Bray. Kristin, who went on to Sandymount High and an academic full-stop, found her own solution when at seventeen-plus she asked me if it was all right if she went to live with John. I said yes, provided there were no children. Agreed.

When Síofra was born, Kristin became her godmother, and that loving relationship, with shifting needs, has endured and deepened and widened to this day. Not so Julian, whose grandmother was his great love, his grandfather his idol, his birth father away. His jealousy of Síofra's arrival in 1971 was palpable and his early hyperactivity became internalised. I began with great hope for a place as Julian's father, but then I began in 1971 to drink again.

The nature of my drinking was different now. I had acknowledged to Douglas Gageby that I was an alcoholic and had done something about it as he suggested. I acquired a new wife, a new career, a new house and a new motor-car. (We were to be a two-car family for 25 years). I had changed everything but myself, and that was because I did not know that I had to change if I was to maintain the measure of serenity that stopping had brought me.

So I slipped back down to the slough of despond, the hollow filled with alcoholic mud. It was a miserable existence because I was pretending to myself and my family that I was not drinking and because this time around I was drinking alone. There was a bottle in the glove compartment; there was a drinks cupboard downstairs; there was wine in the garage and as things got worse there were the early houses, that wonderful Dublin institution which allows dockers and fruitmarket workers and anybody else that needs a drink before the pubs open at 10.30 a.m. to get three hours of heavy drinking done before the first normal face appears in the doorway.

I needed a fix to restore myself to what I saw as normality; to be able to function, use the telephone, make eye contact. There was a little chapel of perpetual adoration on Lower Fitzwilliam Street where I dropped in most mornings towards the end to ask God to ensure that I had enough to see me through to lunchtime. Sometimes this crazy request was granted.

In the first phase of my alcoholism, I drank pints of Guinness and small ones of Jameson Seven. In the second phase, my shadow drinking, to have either of these beverages would be to admit that I really was drinking again. So I took vodka and gin, wine and sherry and port, anything that would exonerate me. So now today you could say that I have not touched whiskey for nearly forty years. But it's alcohol, not whiskey, that is my problem and that is where Alcoholics Anonymous comes in.

I first met AA in St. Patrick's Hospital, where I ended up in May of 1977. I reached rock bottom. By keeping contact with AA and its fellowship, I have not had a drink since then. I know that a drink is an arm's length away. I keep drink in my house and enjoy giving it to family or guests. It is just not for me and I have no problem with the altered attitudes that AA has given me. I see sobriety as a daily gift which I must give away to others in order to keep it. AA is full of paradoxes like that.

You can imagine the destruction that my addiction wreaked on my family. Ostensibly at least, Julian suffered the most. My tongue was my offensive weapon. I can recall a breakfast in Cashel, Kilbride (where we lived for five years). I don't know what led to my remark, but I do sadly remember saying to Julian: "Who could love *you?*".

It was a measure of my own deep unhappiness over those lonely years. I had come to accept my condition as a lifelong imprisonment in the bottle. "The mass of men lead lives of quiet desperation". I knew what Thoreau meant. Who in their right mind could contemplate going back to that? I'll tell you who. I could. I have seen so many people who have thrown away all that I have gained that I have to believe in a daily reprieve, I have to fulfil the simple demands that God makes on me, that AA suggests to me. I have found the *juste milieu* - for today.

And Jenny in all this? It must have seemed like history repeating its disgusting self. She suffered already from depression. Her worst episode was in 1969, in the autumn of the year that began in Beirut. Communication closed off, although we did have a memorable holiday in Italy in 1975. That journey must have sown the seeds of the love we bear today for Mount Amiata in southern Tuscany. I was, I think, confining myself to a beer or two with meals, but it was then that I made my short acquaintance with grappa, a brandy made from the residue of a wine-press. I would slip away to the nearest bar and order a large measure, and then another. I was fooling nobody, but the craving was gruesome.

Jenny survived because she found Al-Anon. Two years before I finally surrendered (I hope), she joined a fellowship that enabled her to detach from me with love. She found hope in the society of other people who were living with the same problem and making independent lives for themselves. It marked a watershed for her and it meant that when I became sick of being sick, she was there for me.

Jenny was on holiday in Kilkee with Síofra and some friends when I entered my last week. I remember a lunch with Professor Louis Cullen in Trinity College. I was a very sick man, barely able to converse with Louis, who must have found me very odd indeed. I remember taking some American friends of Norman and Molly McGrath to Armstrong's Barn at Annamoe. I had Julian with me and again I felt strange and out of this world. The drink was ceasing to work for me.

On 23 May, 1977, I went to Kennedy's, an early house beside Tara Street station. I went for solitude and was surprised to find Seamus Miller, coming off night duty at the Met. Office in O'Connell Street, and an old colleague and friend from *The Irish Times* by the name of Bill Thompson. Within a few days, I was in St. Patrick's Hospital.

When Jenny told her parents that I was in St. Patrick's being treated for alcoholism, they would not believe her. When she told my colleague Seán McQuaid in the Bank of Ireland, he would not believe her. So clever was I at concealment. I did not fall down in drink (except once in London when I was out on the town with Cedric Dickens, (the grandson of), and I was not violent, so by and large I got away with a carefully constructed façade of deceit.

I thought until recently that I did not suffer from blackouts. But my sister Sheila now tells me that when we were living in Whitehall Lodge, she fairly frequently found the black head of a friend, now a well-to-do senior counsel, fast asleep in my bed, and sometimes heard me fall flat on the floor in my bedroom. Her room was above mine so she heard everything. She would hear me carefully put the family Vanguard away; come down, wake me and urge me into bed. That was in the early 1950s, so you can see that I had a long run at the bottle. I reckon now that I was alcoholic from the start, but analysis and blame are poor bedfellows for me. I like the life I have now.

CHAPTER 26

DEV'S MESSAGE

Before I left *The Irish Times* in 1970, I went with Horace Denham of the advertising department to report on the state of the Netherlands. We planned a big supplement but the advertising was not there so it did not happen. We spent at least a week in The Hague (a sleepy city where dinner at seven was out of the question - much too late for the good burghers) and in Amsterdam, where life went on into the small hours.

In The Hague, the great pleasure for me was to meet Eoin MacWhite, the Ambassador, and his wife, Cathy. Eoin was killed in a motor-car accident near his house not long afterward. He was a scholarly man whose father Michael had been in the diplomatic corps before him, and he was a great talker. When I asked him about the small rugs scattered on the carpet of the circular drawing room, Eoin said they were to conceal worn patches. The ceiling was lit by concealed neon tubes and when one went, it often took months to get a replacement from the Board of Works. He was unfortunate in his mileage allowance, for which the minimum was fifty miles. His work took him to Amsterdam, Rotterdam and Utrecht, all of which were about 49 miles away. So he could claim no expenses. Indeed he estimated that he and Cathy had in the previous year spent £1,000 of their own money over and above his salary on maintaining the mission. I hope his successors fared better.

I had a list of articles ready to discuss with Eoin. One was an interview with the Minister for Foreign Affairs. By the next morning, through Eoin's influence, I was in the office of the Deputy Foreign Minister and briefly met his very tall boss, Dr. Joseph Luns, who later became a powerful Secretary-General of NATO. An interview with the Minister of Civil Aviation produced the following encounter:

D.O'D.: Why did you go to school at Clongowes?
Minister: Because I was fucked out of every Jesuit college in the Netherlands. And you can quote me on that.

I had an item on my list which I had called something like " The experience of Irish women married to Dutch husbands". Eoin said sharply: "Well, you can forget that one. More than half of my time is spent unravelling these marriages. It appears that the Dutch family does not open its heart to foreigners that arrive in its midst". That scene is one that I feel has changed for the better in the intervening years.

As a result of the Arms Crisis, I joined Fianna Fáil. I had always believed that it was wrong for a journalist to belong to a political party. My new career at the Bank of Ireland gave me a new freedom, and in The O'Rahilly cumann we (Jenny joined too) made some good friends. I recall with special fondness Sergeant Pat Cleary, a big bluff Kerryman retired from the Garda. Pat was the Lugs Brannigan of Bray, widely known for his rough justice. One tale he told me was of a young delinquent whom he caught thieving in Greystones. Pat made the boy take off his shoes, confiscated them and made the young fellow walk home to Bray in his bare feet. He was much loved and although he often sat with me in the Shillelagh, I knew that he knew that I should not be drinking. We often made the National Collection together, a task that was arduous and tiring but ultimately rewarding for the knowledge it gave me of the Bray seafront and its motley inhabitants.

After Pat died, I did the collection with Connie O'Brien, a Cumann na mBan member from the War of Independence days and still mercifully with us. Connie too I associate with walking. About 1922, she and a group of girls would sometimes go dancing in Glenealy hall. They would think nothing of walking home to Shankill in the early morning. Connie and I ventured far from Bray a few times; once to a party function in Baltinglass. On the way home I had to stop the car at the Wicklow Gap to sleep off the feed of liquor I had taken. She was less concerned than Pat Cleary, but she did not know the extent of my problem.

Fianna Fáil was a bit like the F.C.A. where the more I rose up the ranks the more paperwork had to be done. The higher I rose in the ranks of the Spear Carriers, the less happy I was about the knives that were stuck in my back. Jenny

Brigid O'Donovan about 1975, after Jenny "discovered" her.

would have to wait until 2 a.m. to hear the latest story of blood on the floor of Lawless's Hotel in Aughrim, where our Comhairle Dáil Ceanntair meetings were held.

When Charles Haughey gained office as Taoiseach in 1979, I stayed on too long. I had stopped drinking over two years earlier and I should have reviewed the madness earlier. Jim Ruttle's brief tenure as a Taoiseach's nominee to the Senate was partly my doing, but I took little pleasure from it because Haughey took so long to confirm the appointment.

Political life did not suit me and when I left the Bank of Ireland in 1981, I took advantage of the fact that there was a cumann meeting that night - 9 June - to announce my resignation and the fact that I would be returning to journalism.

When de Valera died in August 1975, a television tribute was paid by John A. Costello, the former Taoiseach. It was an uncharacteristically ungenerous performance, and when six months later Costello himself died, the Opposition tribute was given by Jack Lynch. It was in such contrast to Costello's words on de Valera that I wrote to Lynch, to get this reply:

Dear Donal,
Thank you for your letter commending me on the tribute I paid to John A. Costello. I admit that, to some extent, I had to bite my tongue because of the ungracious comment he made about Dev. Like you I attributed that to some extent to his illness which must have progressed considerably at that time . . .

The car is de Valera's; the biting cold is mine. The President just retired, attended the annual Childers Commemoration ceremony at Glasnevin in November 1973. The Rolls-Royce Silver Wraith with landaulette body by Hooper, was simply known as "Dev's Rolls", though it was built in 1948, registered in 1949, and therefore first served as a State car for President Seán T. O'Kelly. The Government allowed de Valera to use it until his death in 1975.

I was fortunate enough to meet de Valera properly before he left office in 1973. A year before that, I wrote asking him to receive Jenny, Julian and myself. It was a brilliantly hot day in his study and in spite of his blindness he noticed two things. First, what a pleasant day it was in his Presidential gardens; and secondly, how agitated I was by Julian's hyperactive inspection of everything in the room:

"Ah leave him alone, won't you. Sure he's only young".

He concluded the interview by turning to me: "Would you say something to your father from me? Tell him I hope there's no bitterness in his heart towards me as there certainly is no bitterness in my heart towards him".

We drove from Áras an Úachtaráin to Rathgar to deliver Dev's message. My father would not speak to me for four days. His bitterness lived on and he felt a sense of shame, perhaps, that his son would treat with the enemy. Out of this incident de Valera emerged in my eyes the bigger man. Two years later, Dev was dead. I queued with the thousands who wanted to see him lying in state.

Talking to Eoin (The Pope) O'Mahony

As I write these words, I am still full of the feelings generated a couple of days ago by Neil Jordan's film "Michael Collins". A cinematic tour de force, a thrilling drama, a revelation of history, but flawed for me by the implication that the Long Fellow was involved in the killing of the Big Fellow.

CHAPTER 27

FATHER JERRY

O ne of the ways in which Jenny was making a life of her own was highly rewarding for her. She decided to research the life of my great-uncle, Gerald O'Donovan the novelist. This was about the time that Peter Costello began to revive the current interest in him, and was to lead not to a book on "Father Jerry", as we call him in the family, but to the discovery of his living family and a warm friendship with his daughter Brigid.

Costello made a useful contribution to knowledge about Gerald in "The Heart Grown Brutal"[55] and since then John Ryan of Galway has added to our store of information by writing his M.A. thesis in University College Galway; his lively introduction to the Brandon reprint of "Father Ralph", [56] and his extensive and scholarly illustrated essay in the *Journal of the Galway Archaeological and Historical Society*[57]. I paid my own tribute to my father's strange uncle in *Ireland of the Welcomes*[58], where I wrote an article on Loughrea Cathedral and the Celtic Revival for that pioneering editor, Elizabeth Healy.

From the strangest source came a moving tribute to Gerald O'Donovan. Frank Harris (1855-1931) was Irish. He talks in his autobiography of living in Kingstown, holidays in Kerry, education in Galway, Belfast, Carrickfergus and the Royal School at Armagh. An American scholar, John F. Gallagher, edited and wrote the sympathetic introduction to the Grove Press edition of "My Life and Loves", [59] and tells us that "had Frank Harris died in 1914 . . . he would be known to us first as the incomparable Editor of the *Saturday Review* and friend of Oscar Wilde, and then as a writer . . . We would be amused by his rags to riches story and we would like his standing up to Cecil Rhodes and the British

Government in support of the Boers . . .

"But the memory of Frank Harris, in so far as it now exists [in 1963] is drawn from his last fifteen years . . . His books have been out of print in England and America for almost thirty years. Because of its erotic passages, 'My Life and Loves' has long been 'must' reading for tourists in Paris, where it has been in print. Unfortunately, such readers have rarely been disposed to read more than the erotic parts, and there is no gainsaying the impression they have taken away of Harris as a 'sexual gymnast' . . ."

This then is the man and the book in which one of Gerald O'Donovan's novels is called entrancing. Harris writes:

Every now and then a new book brings me to wonder. Some four years ago . . . I received "The Holy Tree . . ." and was carried off my feet. After finishing it, I wrote some reviews of it declaring that it held more of the spirit of true love than any book I had ever read. But my praise seemed lost in the void and was not taken up by anybody.

The other day I opened the book again to see if my praise had been over-strained and almost came to the conclusion that the book must have been written by a woman and an Irish woman at that: it is super-excellent. My school days in Ireland had taught me that there was far more affection, far more pure love, in Ireland than in England, and the belief solves a problem that has tormented many minds. It is known that Cromwell's soldiers, planted here and there in Ireland in order to represent English ideas, were converted to the Irish view very quickly. In a single generation the Ironsides became more Irish than the Irish.

. . . .[H]ere, for the first time in my life, I find a book which gives me this spirit of love in its very essence, and gives it as a readable story; to me an entrancing book. Boni and Liveright [of New York], the publishers, tell me that all they know about Gerald O'Donovan is that he was an Irish priest who had a various and adventurous life and later worked for Lord Northcliffe in London.

From internal evidence I have been able to work out that Frank Harris wrote this, the last volume (V) of "My Life and Loves", in 1930. By then it was eight years since Gerald wrote his last novel. Harris had written twenty conventional books and did not begin his autobiography until he was sixty-five. The book, he says, brought him from comparative wealth to poverty.

Who was this man that Jenny exposed for us? His portrait, by Dermod O'Brien PRHA, was Jenny's wedding present to me. The Pope O'Mahony (Eoin O'Mahony, Barrister-at-Law) was a friend of mine. More accurately, that generous genealogist numbered me among his countless friends. He attended the auction of Dermod O'Brien's widow's effects in 1968, two years before his death, and in a state of great excitement came to tell me that Gerald O'Donovan's portrait had been sold to a dealer in Ranelagh for £7. Nobody except Eoin knew who the subject of the unsigned painting was. Anyway, whatever she had to pay for it, Jenny obtained the portrait and it hangs on our wall still. I estimate the date at 1903, a time when O'Brien painted the pictures of other leaders of Horace Plunkett's co-operative movement.

We were all from West Cork originally. The O'Donovans I mean. Either from West Cork, County Kilkenny or Limerick. "The O'Donovans of Breachna, Desertserges, near Bandon", says Ryan[60], "were tenant farmers on the estate of the Earl of Bandon with a holding of 68 acres". Father Jerry, christened Jeremiah, was born in Newry Street, Kilkeel, Co. Down, where his father, also Jeremiah, was a clerk of works on the building of the pier. The family moved four or five times, wherever piers were to be built, and Jeremiah received his secondary schooling at Ardnaree College, Enniscrone, Co. Sligo.

He entered Maynooth in 1889 when he was eighteen and was ordained in 1895. His second curacy was at Loughrea, Co. Galway, in the diocese of Clonfert. Loughrea, where he was to stay until he left for good in 1904, was a town of "squalor, poverty and chronic wretchedness", to quote Bishop Healy, who noted that its population had declined in living memory from 8,000 to 3,000 (in 1900).

I shall have to move my priestly uncle on more quickly. He was involved in everything - the co-operative movement, for which with Father Tom Finlay S.J., he made a fund-raising tour of the United States; the Gaelic League; the St. Brendan's Total Abstinence Society, which he founded; the Irish Literary Theatre, which he brought from Dublin to perform in the town, and St. Brendan's Cathedral. He was treasurer of the building committee and with Edward Martyn, enlisted the best artists of the Celtic Revival in the cathedral's decoration. He raised funds from America again and was appointed Administrator (Parish Priest) of Loughrea in 1902.

But he was not popular with the Church. He was seen as autocratic and as more fond of consorting with Lady Gregory and her friends than of pastoral work in a poor parish. He fell foul of the new bishop, Dr. O'Dea, and decided to leave. His ultimate standing in the diocese was evidenced by the sincerity of the speakers who expressed the popular regret at O'Donovan's departure in 1904, the year also of James Joyce's self-imposed exile.

The Western News reported:
The scene at the Railway Station when Father O'Donovan was about to depart was a remarkable one. Long before the train started the platform and the road leading from the town were crammed with young and old, anxious to get his blessing before he left, and several knelt on the ground to receive it, and as the train steamed from the station cheer after cheer was raised for the good *soggarth*...

By 1908, he was broke and unfrocked. He had kept up his work for the Gaelic League, though now in London, but he resigned from the committee of the IAOS. On a visit to Donegal to see Hugh Law the Nationalist MP for Donegal, he fell in love with Beryl Verschoyle whom he married in 1910. She was a colonel's daughter and a Fermanagh Protestant. Their first child, Brigid, was the one that Jenny tracked down in London. She had been T.S.Eliot's secretary in Faber and Faber in the 1930s and fell in love with him. But the feeling was not reciprocated and Brigid left. When Jenny first met her, Brigid had just retired as personnel manager of the Design Centre. She had always believed - because her father told her - that he had only one sibling, a brother who had gone down at sea. She was quite astounded to find that Gerald, as he called himself in London, was one of a family of six. She was a warm, loving woman who derived a great pleasure from meeting as many of her family as we could find to greet her in Kilbride Lodge, where later RTÉ recorded a programme on her father.

Gerald wrote six novels, of which "Father Ralph" was the first and arguably the best. It is semi-autobiographical and is a valuable piece of social history. My father was reading a review of it at home in Glasgow in 1913 when he spotted the author's name.

"Is that," he asked his father, "any relation of ours?"
"Give me that!", shouted my grandfather, grabbing *The Catholic Times* and stuffing it into the burning grate.

The black sheep of the family had been erased from the tribal memory. My uncle Dan had, however, a great interest in Gerald O'Donovan. He bought all the novels and had five of them specially bound and printed with his own name, D.J. O'Donovan. God bless the man, he left the lot to me.

I still have to read myself into two further aspects of Gerald's life, his brief commission in the British Army in 1915, and his eventually controversial appointment as Head of British Propaganda in Italy in 1918. But I want to mention his significant liaison with the novelist Rose Macaulay, his secretary in the Italian propaganda department. It was an affair that lasted until his death in 1942. Rose was, says her biographer, Jane Emery [61] "overwhelmed by her responses to his searching mind, his power of sympathy and his sardonic wit". She had fallen "excitingly and painfully in love", and most of her subsequent novels, says John Ryan [62] were influenced by him. In his turn, Gerald wrote his last novel, "The Holy Tree",[63] for Rose. It is clear that Frank Harris knew nothing of Rose Macaulay.

Macaulay's position in the O'Donovan household was always ambiguous. She came to lunch almost every Sunday, did the crossword almost daily by telephone with Gerald, went on long holidays with him and, because she was an appalling driver, was the cause of the severe head injuries he sustained in a motor-car accident in the Lake District in 1937. (Gerald and Rose: Dan and Ursula, in the same area at about the same time).

Beryl chose to ignore the anomaly, but she left Rose out of her diary and noted Gerald's death only with "Gerald left me in the morning" (26 July 1942). Rose ended an anonymous tribute in *The Times* with: "To know him was to love him".

CHAPTER 28

LETTER OF FREEDOM

I don't want you to think that all my efforts and all my years at the Bank of Ireland were wasted. I can summon up with pleasure the active sponsorship of Slógadh, the countrywide competition of youth in music. Much travelling and talk with musicians young and old ensued. I had a memorable conversation with Séamus Ennis (1919-1982), the uilleann piper who in McRedmond's dictionary [64] "occupies a unique role in the history of Irish traditional music in the 20th century because of the extent and diversity of his contribution . . . he was also a whistle player, a singer and storyteller, and a collector of music, song and folklore of priceless cultural importance".

Comhaltas Ceoltóirí Éireann was another institution to which the Bank lent support. For a week or so in a very cold February, I accompanied a group of traditional musicians to Britain. St. Helen's, Newcastle, Leeds and Glasgow were on our itinerary, and in the draughty unheated bus hired from the cheerful Seamus Bourke of Toomevara, who also drove, I can see the faces of Joe Burke the accordion player; P.J. Hernon's brother Máirtín, and Mary Penney of the dancing toes. Paddy Fallon was the M.C. and joke-teller. He had a barber's shop in Drumcondra and a great gift for making the Irish exile laugh. In this way too, I got to know Labhrás Ó Murchú, a man for whom my admiration and respect are undiminished. Belgrave Square in Monkstown is where his monument the Cultúrlann lies.

During my time with the Bank, the new head office building was topped out and occupied. R.K.C. Pilkington was the man charged with setting up systems and allocating the space. Early on I asked Dickie, a plummy-voiced gentleman of the old school, whether he would consider building in a meditation room.

His reply was illuminating:

First, Donal, you have to accept that I am an atheist, so there will be no room with divine connections. Secondly, every floor will have at least one committee room, so that if two people are at odds with each other, they can bind up their wounds in isolation.

My concern was that personal arguments or disagreements could be worked out by separation, so his plan met my request. I had heard that in the main television building at RTÉ, two people who had had a row could too easily meet each other again in the single corridor of the offices.

The architect of Baggot Street was the architect of Montrose. Scott Tallon Walker was the firm, but it was Michael Scott who designed the first and principal television building at Donnybrook and Ronnie Tallon whose name is firmly linked with the strong, timeless, glass-walled design of both. The influence of Mies van der Rohe is clearly stamped on both buildings, though my personal preference is for the Bank of Ireland.

There is a reason. About 1972, I went to New York to see to the press side of the opening of the bank's first office there. When I saw the Seagram Building

A new idea for Ireland, the travelling bank. Photographed by Ian Finlay in Enniskerry, the bank is being patronised by me while Julian eats an ice-cream. About 1973.

on Park Avenue, I gasped. Here, I thought, was the cleanest, crispest expression of modern office architecture that I had seen. I learned that the architect was Mies and the building was not, as I estimated, about two years old, but fifteen. I was mightily impressed and I applauded the bank's choice, which obviously was linked to what had just been completed in Baggot Street. I know that some Georgian buildings and an atmospheric old pub had to be demolished, but there is a powerful argument for good design that moves us and our perceptions on.

One of my better jobs for the bank was to open up the ground floor for various kinds of exhibition, and for use as a marketplace for the composers of Ireland. It was fascinating to wander about from booth to booth listening to the latest work by Jim Wilson or Seoirse Bodley.

I tried concerts too, from jazz to the Consort of St. Sepulchre, but the acoustics were wrong. I took Charles Acton's advice on baffles and placing platforms and chairs, but nothing worked.

Early on in Bill Finlay's Governorship, we invited the Taoiseach, Jack Lynch, as our guest of honour at some function in Baggot Street. Bill and I waited at the top of the steps to greet Lynch, which we thought was observing the right protocol. But it was a dark winter's night and there is a walk of 150 yards from the street to the main door. When he reached us the Taoiseach said:
"That was the longest walk of my life".

He was right of course. Anybody could have attacked him from any one of a number of vantage points. From then on, we went down to the pavement to welcome our guests.

Later in my loose reign, I acceded to a proposal by Seamas Daly that the Bank should give £10,000 to an exhibition of photographs of Ireland to be shown in the National Gallery of Beijing. It was a bold decision but I knew that the Bank was within months of sending a mission to open up the huge potential of that now unsealed society and, to be honest, I welcomed the opportunity of seeing China.

The exhibition, opened by the Irish Ambassador, that civilised man John Campbell, and addressed by the Minister of Culture, was a great success and went on to other centres where it received equal acclaim. It was wonderful to watch the people of Beijing, who had to pay 31/2p to get in, queuing up in the early morning, notebooks in hand, to study and sometimes try to copy the

In the Forbidden City, Peking, with Mr. Wu, our guide, and Seamas Daly in 1980.

photographic artistry of Tom Kelly and Seamas Daly, a partnership soon to break up.

The Summer Palace and the Great Wall were among the many sites we visited, and Seamas and Tom were to go on as far as Mongolia to make up a reciprocal show in Dublin. In Tiananmen Square they were taking down the portraits of Mao Tse Tung (or whatever they call him now, the author of the Little Red Book that we eagerly studied when we were younger). But I wanted to see a farm, and that posed a difficulty. After a few days we were taken to a vast communal enterprise where the (Peking) ducks were force-fed, shepherded down to the river by a skilled dog for exercise, and when they were ready, killed (I didn't see this part); where the workers' small houses had television sets that had no guts; where the beds were made of concrete and heated by bricks slipped underneath, and where the happy schoolchildren sang "Ba Ba Black Sheep" at the teacher's command.

I did not like what I saw of Beijing. The pandas were scrawny, the zoo was undergreened, the people were too many and, in my limited circle of State officials, too greedy. John Campbell gave a splendid dinner for us, but it was spoiled for me by the whingeing and begging of our Chinese hosts who had no idea of the limits of a PR man's budget.

"When", asked Douglas Gageby, "are you going to get rid of that troglodyte

Ryan?" John Ryan of the Power's Whiskey family succeeded Donal Carroll as Governor of the Bank of Ireland. It was during the strike of 1970 that Douglas made that remark, and there was damn all I could do to move Ryan or anybody else. He was succeeded by W.D. Finlay, a man of great sensitivity with a well-stocked mind and, as befitted an eminent senior counsel and academic lawyer, a great ability to think on his feet. It was his great-uncle Father Tom Finlay SJ, who had accompanied my great-uncle Gerald on the begging-bowl tour of America about 1902, when they sought funds for Sir Horace Plunkett's co-operative movement.

It was Bill Finlay himself, and this is not well known, who did the brilliant donkey-work for Hall's history of the Bank of Ireland [65] in 1946. He was a junior counsel then and deserves our thanks for work well done. His brief was "to copy, calendar and index the relevant contents of the Court Minute Books which have been preserved complete from the foundation of the bank" in 1783.

Walter J.P. Curley, the American Ambassador, presenting a bust of Benjamin Franklin (centre) to Dr. William D. Finlay, Governor of the Bank of Ireland. The setting is the House of Lords, College Green part of the Old Parliament House visited by Franklin. The Bank, which acquired the House in 1802 was celebrating the bicentenary of the American Revolution in 1776. Jean-Antoine Houdon (1741-1828) executed this bust in 1778.

When it became clear to me that my well-paid job was giving me no satisfaction whatever, I got the vital endorsement of my wife for my decision to get out. It was not easy and two good friends in the Bank found it hard to understand why I would throw up a sinecure for such a rebellious concept as job satisfaction. But Jenny could see the unhappiness in me and she felt that no sacrifice was too great if it meant dispelling my discontent. The simplest way to explain a complicated series of events is to give you a copy of the letter I wrote in 1980 after much cogitation and reflection. It was addressed to Bill Finlay and I copied it to five relevant senior executives as well:

Dear Governor,
When the accountants take over, it's time for the rest of us to move on. When I was asked by Donal Carroll to join the Bank 10 years ago, I was full of ideas, enthusiasm and energy. Years of unread reports and memos, unheard pleas to get me out from under Raffe Roberts, the dead hand of caution (prudence?) and the slow but crushing realisation that an "outsider" (the word is freely used and accepted in the organisation) can never be allowed into the club - these factors combined to drain the drive out of me.

And then came John Neiland [Director of Planning and Marketing]. A breath of fresh air, I thought. Now we'll get somewhere. And the threat of Niall Crowley, who seemed actively to want to be Mr. Irish Banking (a post left vacant by Dr. Carroll) led to the summoning up of the managerial will to do some of the things I had been pressing for for years (I recommended T.V. courses for senior management one week after I joined in February, 1970).

So a plan was drawn up and from my point of view the only drawback was that I was not to be the executor of the plan. John Neiland said I was unacceptable to senior management and that the plan would be piloted by someone of "A.G.M. rank or upward" You said the Head of Public Affairs had to be a banker because
a)   only a banker could command the necessary resources and
b)   only a banker would be acceptable to other bankers

But, you said, there would be a satisfying and challenging role for me in the new structure and I would have more and easier access to the top than before.

I decided not to involve my union, the National Union of Journalists, but to give the new structure a fair trial. That was in January.

Hilary Hough prepared a release announcing his appointment. No mention of me, Sean McQuaid, Jim Whitty, none of whose appointments was ever publicised. I managed to get a paragraph tagged on saying that I had been appointed Chief Information Manager, whatever that means. At least it saved a little face, but it was not offered: it was extracted.

The release was read by the Chairman to a meeting of the NUJ the day after it reached the papers, after which I was asked to comment. I gave the meeting a brief outline of what had changed and the branch committee decided to seek a meeting with the bank at which they would call for the situation to be "frozen". Laudable but pointless. But now the Bank knows the NUJ exists, has enormous power (e.g. to black copy emanating from the Bank) and will soon have a chapel in the bank to contend with.

In the meantime, it has become crystal clear to me that the Bank of Ireland has wasted 10 years of my life and I now want to retire with what shreds of dignity and honour I can gather about me. I shall need a pension on which to sustain the life of myself and my family (though obviously I shall seek employment in the world of journalism); and I shall need the most generous arrangements possible to be made in regard to my house, my car and my Bank Shares.

I have borne this (to quote John Neiland) "blow between the eyes" since last November 8th, and I have now had enough. Let me go in peace.

It was the best day's work I had done for years. Jenny and I went to Austria for a week and I returned to find that a most generous package had been put together for me. "All I would ask", said John Neiland, "is that you would tell your friends in the Bank that you think it *is* a generous arrangement. They have worked hard for you for the past week and the package has made several trips upstairs to seek improvements". I had no difficulty with that request and I only wish I could name the people who did so much work to ease my departure. I left, as I have said, on 9 June 1981, and as a Christmas box received this touching letter from Bill Finlay:

> . . . I think you know how much I enjoyed working with you in the Bank of Ireland and I am very happy that your decision to practise your profession again independently is one which was taken with

good will on both sides.

My best wishes to you for the future, which I hope will be both agreeable to you and prosperous.

I was, as Jerry Dempsey had said of Desmond Fennell fifteen years earlier, "an experiment that failed". But what a glorious failure!

CHAPTER 29

FLYING COLUMN

I was free. Dread was replaced by hope. I could do what I loved doing most. My meeting with Douglas Gageby was encouraging. "There is plenty for the freelance to do here", he said.

And so it proved. Supplements on industry and trade, book reviews, a mini-series on men of substance - this included Albert Reynolds and Hugh Coveney - the economy of Northern Ireland, Shannon (what else?) and a dozen other subjects. It did not matter what. I was writing again.

The article I was most proud of was not in *The Irish Times*, but in *Studies*[66], an academic harbour in which I never dreamed I could drop anchor. For Pat O'Connell SJ, the Editor, I reviewed Robert Hogan's Dictionary of Irish Literature[67]. It was the lead review and it was about an important book. I was pleased to have pride of place over all the professors and theologians, to be in such distinguished company at all.

Better was to come. A year or so after I took up my pen again, Bill Murdoch, business editor of *The Irish Times*, asked me if I would like to write a weekly column in the business pages. It was to lighten the Monday page, to write about "People in Business" and to cover the world. I could not in my wildest dreams have had a more exciting offer.

I made a mistake by not using my own name on the column. I had the choice and I opted for "Mercator", the pen-name I had used in the 1950s. "Mercator" was a little remote, though of course Jackie Donnelly of the Berkeley

Court Hotel was quick to unmask me. The column began uncertainly, but it soon settled down to featuring a major piece about one person and usually a tailpiece. I had a small expense account, but to get out of Ireland I had to rely on Aer Lingus to fly me gratis.

To move Mercator farther afield than the destinations served by Aer Lingus, I had to make other plans. Peter Britton, the bright young accountant who joined the bank about the time I did and left after me, for a time shared the same room with me in Hume House, Ballsbridge. We got on well and had the benefit of previous experience to get us through the financial and bureaucratic fog. Peter, I would have to say, assimilated better than I. He has a keen sharp mind spiced with a healthy cynicism that I lack.

Remembering Peter's masterly handling of a late 1970s crisis in Masstock, the international farm systems company working then mainly in Saudia Arabia, I decided to ask him if he could organise a visit to the Kingdom for me. Using his contacts, Peter put together a package through which Masstock, the ESB, McInerneys the builders and CTT shared the cost of transporting and accommodating me to and in Jeddah, Ryadh, Dhahran and a number of lesser-known places in that vast landscape.

I'm talking of March-April 1984, and I'm talking of the power and influence of Irish enterprise in a political and economic minefield. Alastair McGuckian was the managing director of Masstock Saudi and the master mind who built an empire in the Kingdom. At the time I wrote:

> You have to picture me with Alastair as he talks. We are sitting on a bale of hay surrounded by fields of green wheat 100 miles out from Ryadh. The wheat belongs to one of Masstock's 23 cereal farms and the cheese which forms the mainstay of our picnic is one of the dozens of products marketed throughout Saudi Arabia by Almarai, a company 50 per cent owned by Masstock International, itself 100 per cent owned by Alastair and his brother, Paddy. The other half of Almarai is owned by Prince Sultan Bin Mohamed Bin Saud Al Kabir and thereby hangs a tale which will have to wait for another day.

The tale that was hanging then is so far as I know, still hanging, but the success went on. The wheat farms were created by erecting huge booms over wells and moving them in circles completed every twenty-four hours. Each boom contains sprinklers that emit a constant supply of water and cause the greening of Saudia Arabia. Of course you can grow grass the same way, so there were ten dairy farms and three milk processing plants with a turnover then of £200 million a year with a staff of 700, a lot of them Irish.

In a world which has very few 1,000-cow dairy farms, Alastair McGuckian and Prince Sultan then held six times that number. And whereas Ireland had then a million cows, Saudia Arabia had about 25,000. I was mighty impressed by that network of industries and by the contracts won in fair fights by McInerneys and the ESB. There were many other Irish people involved in developing the Kingdom. I met a large number of them at a St. Patrick's Day "thrash" (the ex-pats word for a piss-up) held at the Irish Embassy, where it is permissible to ingest alcohol.

Hundreds of memories crowd in on me as I mentally revisit the Kingdom and I thank Peter Britton again for his ingenuity and promptness in responding to my wild dream.

Something I wrote sparked the great General Michael J. Costello to write to me: "I am one of yesterday's men, and my memories are of the past. They are relevant to today only in so far as I have the grim thought : 'I told you so'". Four years later, Costello died and the lengthy obituary was mine. Over the years we had become good friends. The leading article on 22 October 1986 ended: "Ireland has lost a great son" . The writer I suspect was Captain Douglas Gageby (retd.)

Pushing out the boundaries of the business world was what I enjoyed most about writing the Mercator column. I could write about Sam Stephenson the architect. "It is not too fanciful", I wrote in 1982, "to link the names of James Gandon and Sam Stephenson, for the one set his unique stamp on the Dublin of 1780 to 1800 and the other is making his distinctive mark on the 20th century city". We should not forget Sam. His Central Bank, his part of the Civic Offices, his Bord na Móna building in Baggot Street, his EBS offices in Westmoreland Street - these and the controversial ESB offices in Lower Fitzwilliam Street of which Raymond McGrath [68] so heartily approved, will remain when we are all gone. They make a statement about the way we were in the later decades of the century. Arthur Gibney, for many years Sam's partner, finished Raymond McGrath's design for the Royal Hibernian Academy and was the architect of the Irish Management Institute building and others quite as distinguished.

And I wrote about art by talking to collectors such as Vincent Ferguson of

Fitzwilton and Gordon Lambert of Jacobs, about whom I quoted "a very senior member" of the Department of Foreign Affairs as saying: "What Tony O'Reilly has done for business, Gordon Lambert has done for art. He has broken through to a world of Rockefellers and Mellons, a world that is above business, above politics and above ethnic interests".

Writing a column gives one a great opportunity to sound off about hobby horses. (There's a nice essay in mixed metaphors for you). One of my pet hates always has been gobbledegook. In this dislike I was joined (metaphorically) by Malcolm Baldridge, the U.S. Secretary of Commerce in 1983. Mr. Baldridge campaigned against "the multisyllabic jargon and verbal distortions which increasingly obscure the real meaning of what is being said or written". He told of a conversation which former Secretary of State General Alexander Haig had with an aide who asked for a pay-rise. Haig replied:

> Because of the fluctuational predisposition of your position's productive capacity as juxtaposed to Government standards, it would be momentarily injudicious to advocate an increment.

"I don't get it", said the aide.

"That's right", said General Haig.

Another of my hobby horses, as you already know, is the county of Clare. I have mentioned Naoise Cleary, long gone to his reward. In *Ireland of the Welcomes*[69] I wrote an article on Naoise's Clare Heritage Centre at Corofin. Now that we are marking the 150th anniversary of the Great Hunger, the Corofin resource seems even more relevant. The centre is in the old church of St. Catherine, donated by the Church of Ireland because they no longer have any members to form a congregation. In 1834 Corofin had 212 Protestants: now there is none.

But the church predates that count. It was built around the bones of a converted barn between 1715 and 1720. By 1820 it had fallen into disrepair and received £36 from the Board of First Fruits (First Fruits were the whole income of an incumbency for the first year). With that and local money a steeple and vestry were added.

"There's no luck in priest's money", was a favourite saying of Naoise Cleary's, though he was referring to the Roman Catholic variety. In Corofin at that time the priests' income was greater than that of any farmer in the parish. Some were charitable: others were rapacious enough.

Between 1851 and 1886, exactly 100,496 people had to quit County Clare for ever and to emigrate mostly to the United States and, from East Clare, to New South Wales. "The calamitous years", as F.S.L. Lyons [70] has said, "burnt themselves into the imagination of the people and have haunted their descendants ever since".

The greatest war that the world has suffered came to an end as the calendar marked the centenary of the Great Famine. Little, therefore, was done to mark the Irish event. Europe had to bind up her wounds. But it is tempting to add that the native scars also needed more time. Only now, after another fifty years, have we been able to look back without anger.

Paul O'Dwyer, the human rights lawyer, featured in my first book, "Dreamers of Dreams: Portraits of the Irish in America". Paul not only welcomed me at very short notice but gave me a serious interview and a copy of his book "Counsel for the Defense" (1979). Born in Lismirrane, Bohola, Co. Mayo, in 1907, he spent his life fighting injustice everywhere.

It was those Clare people and those from the other counties of the West that made possible my first book. I had been to America so often and had met so many Irish Americans that Jim Whitty of the Bank of Ireland suggested publishing a compilation. I went one better. I selected twenty-five distinguished exiles or descendants of exiles and spent seven weeks interviewing them on their now native heath.

Dr. A.J.F. (Tony) O'Reilly

In January 1984 I decided to begin by asking Tony O'Reilly, an old acquaintance since forgot, to set a date around which to corral the rest.

"I'll meet you", said Dr. O'Reilly, "in the Hotel Pierre in New York at 4 o'clock on 22 May". Fair enough: he's a busy man. "Dreamers of Dreams: Portraits of the Irish in America" [71] was on its way.

By the summer of 1984, I was in a quandary. I had finished the manuscript. I knew where it would sell. I had got Professor Joe Lee's introduction.

But there was no sign of Cardinal Tomás Ó Fiaich. I had written to the Primate early in the year and got a gracious reply saying yes, he would be delighted to contribute a foreword. Just send him a few sample chapters and he would put pen to paper.

Time passed. I wrote several times to no effect. Then I telephoned Father Clyne, the Cardinal's secretary. I told him the foreword was urgent, was holding up the publication. I said: "Father, I've taken the liberty of writing a foreword myself. Would you ask His Eminence to sign it?" I thought Clyne might explode.

But: "Donal", he said, "it's your only chance. You have encountered one of the great promisers, a man who will say yes to anything. Today is Friday. Post it now. It'll reach us here tomorrow and you'll have it back signed on Monday".
"But Father", I said, "tomorrow's Saturday".
"Yes, but you're writing to the civilised part of Ireland. We in Armagh have a post on Saturdays".

Well, the outcome was extraordinary - Cardinal Ó Fiaich not only adopted my text *in toto* but there and then, using my style he added twice as much again.

With Sam Stephenson and Dr. Patrick Hillery, President of Ireland.
In Kilkenny Castle where Dr. Hillery accepted a copy of "Dreamers of Dreams", 1984.

Four of the great people who featured in "Dreamers of Dreams". Eoin McKiernan (top left), John Kerry O'Donnell (top right), Kevin Roche (bottom left) and Thomas (Teddy) Gleason (bottom right). The most famous in the Ireland of the 1940s to 1980s was John Kerry O'Donnell, the stormy petrel of the GAA in New York. John was a native of Gleann na nGealt, Camp, Co. Kerry and acquired his first saloon bar in 1935. Eoin McKiernan was the founder and President of the Irish American Cultural Institute. Eoin, a fluent Irish speaker, was the son of a Manhattan-born Irishman. His monument is Éire-Ireland, a quarterly magazine of impeccable standards and consummate interest to students of Irish literature and history. Kevin Roche's father was jailed in the Civil War when he was a T.D. In the belief that "an industrial country is where an architect has to be", Kevin went to America after graduation, joined Eero Saarinen, the leading firm of corporate architects in the United States and soon succeeded to the practice, becoming one of the country's premier architects and winner of the Pritzger Prize. Of these four, the best-known in America was undoubtedly Thomas W. (Teddy) Gleason, President for 25 years of the International Longshoremen's Association and Grand Marshal of the New York St. Patrick's Day Parade in 1984. He led the greatest revolution in port workers' history in 1964-65, a feat which was acknowledged worldwide. Teddy launched the book for me in 1985 at the Irish-American Historical Society's beautiful old premises on Central Park and Fifth. Among the guests was Charles J. Haughey.

He made what turned out to be a most valuable contribution to my poor offering. He gave dignity to what was really a vanity book, and miracles of miracles sent it to me by the Monday.

That book made money for me, made possible by the marketing skills of my friend and partner Seamas Daly. But it did little else. It was a journalist's book, each chapter led by a studio photograph. It served as a vade-mecum for a number of Irish people intent on learning more about the Irish-American scene, usually with dollar signs in their eyes.

It was not until three years later that I began to learn what real research was. I was still writing the Mercator column for *The Irish Times* when the paper decided that after five years they didn't want the column any more.

Jim Dunne, the Editor of *Business and Finance,* had been appointed Senior Finance Editor of *The Irish Times* over Bill Murdoch's head. I wrote to congratulate him. On 14 September, 1987, Jim wrote:

Dear Donal,

Thank you for your recent letter. I'm sorry that my first to you is to tell you that I am retiring "Mercator". One specific task *The Irish Times* has set me is to re-do the Monday business coverage from top to toe. The "Mercator" column is, in my opinion, too gentle and sometimes over-personal - nice qualities in the author of the column, but not conducive to catching the readers' undivided attention.

I thank you for your years of service to the paper. I'm sure that you enjoyed doing the column, and that you made many new friends along the way. I wish you well.

I didn't want Jim Dunne to patronise me like that. Even more, I didn't want to lose my column. A few days later, coming back from a flight to New

With P.V. Doyle and Douglas Gageby at the Irish launch of "Dreamers of Dreams"
in the Berkeley Court Hotel, 1984.
Through the good offices of Michael Governey, the manager, the reception was hosted by P.V. Doyle

York, I saw Jim. He sat in the seat ahead of me and I seriously considered pouring a cup of coffee over his head. But I cooled down after a few weeks and realised that the column had run its course after five rewarding years.

Jenny and I had earlier that year, 1987, made a round-the-world journey, sending the column from four countries and, for me, revisiting India and for both of us seeing Australia, Fiji, Hawaii and Vancouver for the first time.

With Seán MacBride at the "Dreamers of Dreams" launch, Dublin 1984.

We stayed with my brother-in-law Donal O'Sullivan and his wife Una in Brisbane. It was a moving meeting after so many years. In Sydney we were among the last guests to stay at the old Gresham Hotel. We used the Gresham as a base from which to call on all Raymond McGrath's surviving relatives in the Sydney area and on Ken and Rosemary Pye and Wendy and Bill Henningham. Ken and Wendy were the children of Elmo and Ruth Pye, worshippers at the shrine of Raymond McGrath. Pictures by Raymond and sculptures by his sister Eileen lay around like idols and it was good to meet Ruth, a very old lady. Elmo, the faithful family lawyer, was recently dead. I likened Jenny's cousins to yeomen, solid English stock carved out of a previous era. Reliable people, mainly and appropriately called Smith.

But Dan was the highlight of the visit. Dan is a Cistercian monk, son of my diplomat uncle Colman O'Donovan. Because of Dan's upbringing as a migrant, his life as a boarder at Clongowes Wood, and his vocation, we had never met. In recent years we had begun to correspond and by cassette I talked to him about various skeletons in the family cupboard. He had not heard the voice of an O'Donovan since 1962, when he left the mother house at Roscrea to join the new community at Tarawarra Abbey in Victoria.

From there Dan left to become an anchorite in Western Australia. There is a dramatic double-page photograph of him in "A Day in the Life of Australia". He is sitting legs apart outside his tin shed in the desert.

At Dan's ordination as a Cistercian monk, Mount St. Joseph Abbey, Roscrea, 1958. In the back row are Joseph Brennan ("Uncle Joe"), Governor of the Central Bank; Maeve and Louis McRedmond, and my father, Jim. Clockwise from Dan are his mother Moll; his sister Maureen; Ethel O'Donovan (née Bouchier-Hayes); Dorothy O'Donovan (wife of my uncle Dan); Evelyn Simcox, wife of Joe Brennan, and Dan's brother Diarmuid. Above Dan's head is my mother Monty. Beside Dan is his father Colman. The nun is Aunty Matt of the Ursulines in Cork and above her is uncle Peter O'Donovan married to Ethel. - Courtesy of Louis and Maeve McRedmond.

Jenny and I had been so impressed by his letters to us that we decided before we left Ireland that if he turned out to be the person we were reading about, we would ask him to give us his blessing. We had had to marry in a registry office and we always felt there was something missing from the ceremony.

Dan took a bus from Fitzroy Crossing, where he had become the parish priest, ministering to those Aborigines who cared to listen to him. It took him two days to get to Alice Springs, our chosen meeting place.

Father Dan O'Donovan in his hotel room, Alice Springs, 1987.

Jenny and I got the bus from Adelaide, which took 23 hours to get to Alice. We had barely met Dan when we asked him our favour. His assent was instant. We spent two hours that evening at an AA meeting (there was no other meeting for Jenny to go to) and returned to Dan's hotel room to find that he had been preparing himself for his work.

It was a simple, purely spiritual experience. Dan spoke to us, in turn and together, then placed his hand on our heads. I can find no further words to describe how it was. He used no books or bells or candles. He spoke no formal prayers. We did not need to see Ayers Rock. He just was, for us.

Jenny presenting Raymond McGrath's thesis on Chinese Architecture to the Australian National Gallery in 1987. Left is Andrew Sayers, right is Roger Butler, both of the gallery, now headed by Dr. Brian P. Kennedy of the National Gallery of Ireland.

CHAPTER 30

BARRY COUNTRY

"What do I do now?", I asked my daughter Síofra.
"You write a biography", she said.
"About whom?"
"About your father, about Father Jerry, about Kevin Barry", she said.
"If that's the choice", I replied, "I'll settle for Kevin Barry"[72].

It was a fascinating task that I set myself. My father had written an unpublished book on Barry over a period of twenty years. He had, as I discovered, "acquired" the legal papers concerning the court-martial, so I had a mass of unpublished and unique material to work on. Those papers are in the National Library and if my father had not taken them from Dublin Castle in 1921, they would moulder still in the Public Record Office in London. They would, I think, be subject to the 75-year rule that applies to legal papers and would not have been open for inspection until 1995. I never discovered whether Jim O'Donovan captured them before the Truce of July 1921 or stole them in the more peaceful months that followed.

Another extraordinary document that came my way was Kevin Barry's sister's

Síofra from a photograph to illustrate the hair styles offered at Colm Kiely's Upper Cuts salon in Bray, 1989.

testimony to the Bureau of Military History. The Bureau was established in 1947 to record for posterity the actions of those who took part in the War of Independence from 1913 to 1921.

Its records were not to be made public for twenty-five years, a period since extended by various governments. They still have not been released, but close relatives are entitled to a copy of the testimony given by the person concerned. Kathy Barry gave my father extracts from her own testimony, but she withheld the essential fact — told to her by Kevin Barry during a recess in the court-martial — that he had shot a specific soldier with the fourth round fired with his .38 Mauser automatic. This was Private Matthew Whitehead of the 2nd Battalion the Duke of Wellington's Regiment.

I, of course, used this vital piece of information in the book, but under the guidelines for the Bureau of Military History testimony, I could not directly give my source. It is an odd situation. My father, even though he presented three spent bullets to the National Library, didn't know, though he must have suspected, that Kevin Barry had used one of them to kill Whitehead. And his son is not allowed to reveal his source in print. It is high time that the Bureau's buried treasure was opened to the public.

Julian at Kilbride Lodge about 1988.

Papers and records, photographs and letters all form the bones of biography. But to get to the character and personality of Kevin Barry, I had to look elsewhere. His best friend, Air Commodore Gerry McAleer, was a retired Royal Air Force doctor living in England. He was a generous source of history and anecdote over three fruitful nights. Equally helpful were all my cousins and Barry's only surviving sister, Elgin O'Rahilly, the widow of The O'Rahilly.

To get the feel of Barry's physical background, I kept in my mind the experience of Robert A. Caro [73] when he was writing the life of Lyndon Johnson, President of the United States from 1963 to 1968.

With Kristin on Lough Derg c. 1988

Johnson was raised in the Hill Country of Texas. That country covers 24,000 square miles and is as different from Caro's background as it is from the townland of Tombeagh, near Hacketstown, Co. Carlow, where the Barrys come from. The Hill Country's population density then was about one person per square mile and most significantly there was no electricity, therefore no movies, few radios, no water pumps even where some of the wells were seventy-five feet deep. That meant that the women of the house had to haul up and carry about three hundred tons of water, bucket by bucket, every single year.

It took the young congressman more than ten years, but he brought electricity to these people, and they never forgot it, even calling their babies after him. As indeed, the people of Ireland did for a long time after Kevin Barry was hanged.

Robert Caro began his research by flying occasionally from his native New York City to Austin, Texas, and then hiring a car to drive into the Hill Country, properly called Edwards Plateau.

It soon began to dawn on him that the culture there was so different from his own that he would have to do something drastic. One day he said to his wife Ina: "I'm not really understanding these people, or Lyndon Johnson. We have to move to the Hill Country". So for parts of three years he lived there with his wife, talking to the people who made up Johnson's first political machine.

The dark side of Johnson's life would never have come to light if Caro had not immersed himself in the life of the Hill Country.

He had some very unproductive interviews with Lyndon Johnson's brother Sam Houston, who was an alcoholic. The point came when Caro stopped talking to him because his stories were unreliable and not usable in the book.

Then one day, a couple of years on, Caro encountered Sam Houston in the streets of Johnson City. What he met was a changed man. Sam Houston Johnson had had cancer. He had stopped drinking. He was serene in himself and he had become religious. Caro tried again.

When the tourists had left the old Johnson homestead for the day, Caro said: "Now Sam Houston, sit down in your seat and re-create for me one of those terrible arguments that your father used to have with Lyndon".

Sam Houston began to speak, slowly at first, then faster and faster. When, acting his father at the head of the table, he shouted: "Lyndon, God damn it, you're a failure, you'll be a failure all your life", Caro said to him: "Now Sam Houston, I want you to tell me all the stories about your brother's boyhood that you told me before, the stories that your brother told all those years, only give me more details".

There was a long pause. Then Sam Houston said: "I can't". Caro asked: "Why not?" He said: "Because they never happened".

Nothing so dramatic occurred when I was researching "Kevin Barry", though one woman cousin said: "I know nothing. I remember nothing. My life began when I got married".

I began my research with a visit to the Carlow equivalent of the Hill Country. On January 4th, 1988, I went by myself to stay in a freezing caravan on the Barry family farm. I wanted to soak myself in the fields, the school, the house, the churches and the drinking places that surrounded Kevin Barry's life in Tombeagh.

The family had a house and a dairy business in Dublin, so his other life was more accessible to me. I could understand and share a middle-class urban upbringing, education and pursuits. I knew little of life in the countryside fifty miles from the city.

I chose not to stay in the Barry house because I wanted to breathe the air he breathed in isolation. The farm is now run by my cousin, also Kevin Barry, and I later stayed there with my wife Jenny. We felt the ghosts and we heard the silences that for my mother's people formed the stuff of evening entertainment. You won't believe it but that house, Tombeagh, was not electrified until 1959, nearly 300 years after it was built and forty years after Barry was hanged. It was Kevin's brother Michael who eventually installed the electric current.

The Barry book, launched by Charlie Haughey in the Kevin Barry Room in the old UCD at Earlsfort Terrace, was published by Glendale Press. The owner, Tom Turley, was a good editor but a bad businessman. Between hopping and trotting, I made no money out of the book and Tom went out of the publishing business. But I'm glad I wrote it and was able to straighten out a few wrinkles in the family's perception of Kevin. It got a good press here and in America.

CHAPTER 31

GOD'S ARCHITECT

After Kevin Barry, what? Jenny suggested that I attempt a life of her father Raymond McGrath. If I had known what lay ahead, I would surely have refused. But I did not envisage six years' work and travel to Australia, America, England and France, as well as months of research and reading at home.

The beginning was Seamas Daly's. I asked how I should proceed and he said: "First write the book. Then take Nick Robinson out to the most expensive lunch possible at a restaurant he likes. Then seek his advice".

At Patrick Guilbaud's, Nick was decisive: "Two things are essential: first get the funds together - sponsorship, grant-aid, loans, whatever it takes. Secondly, get the book designed before going near a publisher. In that way you get the book you want and no cutting down on quality, design or the number of pictures you want to include".

That lunch was a real investment. Nick had founded the Irish Architectural Archive with Eddie McParland of Trinity and thus was the recipient of one of the Archive's first collections. Jenny had given the Archive the bulk of her father's papers, drawings, sketches, notebooks in 1978. Nick himself has been an admirer of McGrath's work for a long time and has several of his pictures. He was gracious enough to contribute a foreword to the book and of course he was able, because he is married to President Mary Robinson, to write:

And here McGrath's path crosses my own again. His alterations at Áras an Uachtaráin are individually elegant and, in that historic context, evidence of McGrath's principled commitment to the twentieth century.

"God's Architect" [74] became my life. When I got to Australia, I found that two men there had begun to work on biographies of McGrath. One was John Warnock, the well-known Australian broadcaster. John was 45 when he died of cancer a few months before I arrived. His father Bob most generously gave me all the work John had done.

Then I had to tackle Andrew Metcalf, who in 1990 was a busy architect in private practice in Sydney. We met on Anzac Day and from his window together watched the local bowling club stand to attention for the Anthem played by a large brass band. I couldn't see any band and Andrew had to explain to me that we and the bowlers were listening to a tape. Andrew had not done as much work on McGrath as John Warnock, but he was an accomplished writer on architecture and he asked if he could contribute an analysis of Raymond's work. But he had not been to Europe, had not seen the work and could not have written what eventually Alan Powers of London, the biographer of Oliver Hill, was able to contribute. After talking for four hours, we parted friends.

When I blithely say "got to Australia" I have to explain that at Seamas Daly's suggestion I had sought and got a travel and research grant from the then Córas Tráchtála, the Export Board. CTT was enlightened enough to see a book as an export and so in 1989 and again in 1990 I was able to work abroad, wisely and soberly expending £10,000 of the taxpayer's money. It was a great privilege and I am grateful for it.

My visit to France was amusing and sad. Jean Stempowski was an old friend of Jenny's parents. Well, of Mary's really: he found Raymond difficult to communicate with. He was a small retired cotton merchant from Le Havre. Having spent six months at an English public school, he was a compleat Anglophile. Jenny and I knew him in Paris, where he had a wife, four children and a mistress, Tootie, whom I got to know over several visits. My last sight of her was in Les Halles. She had just been told that Jean was retiring to St. Raphaël on the Côte d'Azur, and she was very upset.

"You are discarding me like an old glove", she told Jean over dinner, with me listening. (She worked in a glove shop off the Rue de Rivoli). His assurances of fixed meetings did not mollify her, but in fact they did meet once a year at Avignon. Tootie at 52 retired to her native Vevey, leaving Switzerland to house the only two mistresses I had known in my life.

Jean and his eccentric daughter Jacqueline were expecting me at the Villa Tanit. But there was no sign of his elderly wife Suzanne. She had been taken ill for the first time in her life and was in hospital. Then came dinner time. Neither Jean at 85 nor Jacqueline at 60-plus had ever cooked anything. They were helpless and hungry, so I suggested omelettes. They told me where most things were, but I had to join them in the search for butter and salt and pepper.

Half an hour and three unsuitable pans later, I had three passable omelettes on three warmed plates. I don't remember what else I gave them but we didn't go short.

Poor Suzanne lived on until she was 96 and Jean who was younger, survived her by a little. Jacqueline still lives in St. Raphaël but the Villa Tanit is in other hands.

Aer Lingus got me to the United States and enabled me to meet such great people as the frail and elderly Hazel Guggenheim in New Orleans, where I saw a portrait of her famous father, Benjamin, one of the victims of the iceberg that struck the *Titanic*. And Serge Chermayeff, the Russian-born architect who had worked with McGrath and Wells Coates on the interior design of Broadcasting House in London in 1930-32.

Serge, who died in 1996, was also elderly and I suppose frail, but the word doesn't suit a man of such strong opinions and loud voice. He was quite deaf and when his wife Barbara tried to put in her tuppence-worth would shout: "Shut up, Barbara. He doesn't want to hear that". I spent three happy days on Cape Cod with that couple and their flea-ridden dog. Barbara was most kind, driving me here and there in her Jeep Cherokee and filling in the gaps that Serge had left. He was one of a kind, a formidable man whom I met too late to establish any sort of relationship. "God's Architect" - the title comes from a dream that McGrath had while he was at Cambridge - was enjoyable to research and write. Phase II was to get it designed and here, at Nick Robinson's suggestion, I went to Ted and Ursula O'Brien, the Cork couple who were doing wonderful work in Dublin designing books for the Architectural Archive, for Eoin O'Brien's Black Cat Press and for many others. They are such a delight to work with that I often wondered when we were going to have a row. We still haven't had it because like the printers they prefer to work with, Bairds of Antrim, they are dedicated professionals.

Those six years sped past and the result was a large-format book of 357 pages and about 400 illustrations. It was partly backed by the Office of Public Works who arranged a launch in Dublin Castle where we stood in July 1995 on one of Raymond McGrath's beautiful Donegal Carpets. Hugh Coveney, Minister of State at the Department of Finance, was present as Dr. Maurice Craig launched the book. Maurice moved some people to tears with what he said. He is our foremost architectural historian, a writer of elegance, a poet of distinction. And a good friend.

With that book published, with all those good people gathered around me, with my wife and helpmeet Jenny beside me, I might as well say goodbye. I don't want to push my luck.

At the launch of "God's Architect" at Dublin Castle, July 1995.
From left: Hugh Coveney, T.D. Minister of State; Jenny; the author, and Dr. Maurice Craig.

REFERENCES

1. Scott, Canon George Digby. The Stones of Bray. Hodges Figgis, Dublin. 1913.

2. Ball, Dr. Elrington. History of the County of Dublin.

3. Ó Broin, Leon. No Man's Man. Institute of Public Administration, Dublin. 1982.

4. Welch, Robert. The Oxford Companion to Irish Literature. Oxford University Press. 1996.

5. Sheehy Skeffington, Andrée. Skeff: A Life of Owen Sheehy Skeffington. 1909-1970. Lilliput, Dublin 1991.

6. Lucy, John. There's A Devil in the Drum. Faber and Faber, London. 1938.

7. Carter, Carolle J. The Shamrock and the Swastika. Pacific, Palo Alto. 1977.

8. Farrell, James T. On Irish Themes. Ed. Dennis Flynn. University of Pennsylvania Press. 1982.

9. Stephan, Enno. Spies in Ireland. Macdonald, London. 1963.

10. See note 7.

11. Fisk, Robert. In Time of War. Paladin, London. 1983.

12. Farago, Ladislas. The Game of the Foxes. Pan, London. 1973.

13. Duggan, John P. Neutral Ireland and the Third Reich. Gill and Macmillan, Dublin. 1985.

14. Documents on German Foreign Policy 1918-45 Series D Vol. VIII. (HMSO) London 1954. pp 241-2 Hempel to Foreign Ministry 8.10.39.

15.   Andrews, C.S. Man of No Property. Mercier, Dublin 1982.

16.   See note 9.

17.   Cronin, Seán. Frank Ryan: The Search for the Republic. Repsol, Dublin. 1980.

18.   See note 17.

19.   See note 17.

20.   See note 17.

21.   Bell, J. Bowyer. The Secret Army. Sphere London. 1972.

22.   MacEoin, Uinseann. Harry: The Story of Harry White. Argenta, Dublin. 1985.

23.   O'Donovan, Donal. Kevin Barry and His Time. Glendale, Dublin. 1989.

24.   Meenan, James (ed.). Centenary History of the Literary and Historical Society 1855 - 1955. Kerryman, Tralee.

25.   See note 23.

26.   The National Student. New Series no. 105, February 1949. "As you were" p.49.

27.   Hickey, D.J., and Doherty, J.E. A Dictionary of Irish History: 1800-1980. Gill and Macmillan, Dublin. 1980.

28.   The Irish Times, 2 November, 1943. Reprinted in "Times past", 1993.

29.   Ibid. 11 February 1944.

30.   Ireland of the Welcomes Vol. 34 No. 3 May-June 1985 "Seán MacBride - Freedom Fighter to Nobel Prizewinner", by Donal O'Donovan, pp. 22-27.

31.   McRedmond, Louis (ed.) Modern Irish Lives: Dictionary of 20th Century Biography. Gill and Macmillan, Dublin, 1996.

32.   Weston St. John Joyce. The Neighbourhood of Dublin. Hughes and Hughes, Dublin 1994. (First pub. 1912).

33.   Campbell, Michael. Lord Dismiss Us. Heinemann, London. 1967.

34.   Campbell, Michael. Peter Perry. Collier Books, New York. 1961.

35.   The Irish Times. O'R. (The O'Rahilly). June 20, 1979.

36.   See note 9.

37.   See Note 23.

38.   Browne, Noël. Against The Tide. Gill and Macmillan, Dublin. 1986.

39.   Deeny, James. To Cure and to Care, Glendale, Dublin. 1989.

40.   O'Donovan, Donal. God's Architect: A Life of Raymond McGrath.

Kilbride Books, Bray. 1995.

41. Gray, Tony. Mr. Smyllie, Sir. Gill and Macmillan, Dublin 1991.

42. Orr, Charles. Splash!: Drama and Comedy in a Newspaperman's Career. Merlin Books, Devon. 1989.

43. Quoted in Oram, Hugh. The Newspaper Book: A History of Newspapers in Ireland, 1649-1983. MO Books, Dublin. 1983.

44. See note 27.

45. Fogarty, Michael P. Report of Banks Inquiry. Stationery Office, Dublin 1971.

46. Breathnach, Diarmuid and Ní Mhurchú, Máire. Beathaisnéis a Ceathair. An Cló-Chomhar, Átha Cliath. 1995.

47. Teahan, John. The Dr. Kurt Ticher Donation of Irish Silver to the National Museum of Ireland. National Museum, Dublin.

48. Johnston, Denis. Nine Rivers from Jordan. 1953.

49. Oram, Hugh. The Newspaper Book: A History of Newspapers in Ireland, 1649-1983. MO Books, Dublin. 1983.

50. See note 40.

51. Louis McRedmond ed. Modern Irish Lives: Dictionary of 20th-century Irish Biography. Gill and Macmillan, Dublin, 1996.

52. See note 27

53. O'Donovan, Donal. Dreamers of Dreams: Portraits of the Irish in America. Kilbride Books, Bray. 1984.

54. See note 40.

55. Costello, Peter. The Heart Grown Brutal. Gill and Macmillan, Dublin 1977.

56. O'Donovan, Gerald. Father Ralph. Brandon Books, Dingle.1993.

57. Ryan, John F. Journal of the Galway Archaeological and Historical Society. Vol. 48, 1996. pp 1-47.

58. O'Donovan, Donal. Ireland of the Welcomes, Vol. 33 No. 2 March-April 1984. pp 41-45

59. Harris, Frank. My Life and Loves. Grove Press, New York. 1963.

60. See note 57.

61. Emery, Jane. Rose Macaulay: A Writer's Life. John Murray, London, 1991.

62. See note 57.

63. O'Donovan, Gerald. The Holy Tree. Heinemann, London. 1922.

64. See note 51.

65. Hall, F.G. The Bank of Ireland 1783-1946. Ed. George O'Brien with architectural chapter by C.P. Curran and biographical notes by Joseph Hone. Hodges Figgis, Dublin and Blackwell, Oxford. 1949.

66. Studies. Autumn/Winter 1980. Dublin.

67. Hogan, Robert ed. Dictionary of Irish Literature. Gill and Macmillan, Dublin. 1980.

68. See note 40.

69. Ireland of the Welcomes. Vol. 32 No. 3 May-June 1983.

70. Lyons, F.S.L. Ireland Since the Famine. Weidenfeld and Nicolson, London. 1971.

71. See note 53.

72. See note 23.

73. Zinsser, William ed. The Art and Craft of American Biography. Robert A. Caro on "Lyndon Johnson and the Roots of Power". American Heritage, New York. 1986.

74. See note 40.

INDEX